SAGE was founded in 1965 by Sara Miller McCune to support the dissemination of usable knowledge by publishing innovative and high-quality research and teaching content. Today, we publish over 900 journals, including those of more than 400 learned societies, more than 800 new books per year, and a growing range of library products including archives, data, case studies, reports, and video. SAGE remains majority-owned by our founder, and after Sara's lifetime will become owned by a charitable trust that secures our continued independence.

Los Angeles | London | New Delhi | Singapore | Washington DC | Melbourne

ADVANCE PRAISE

It's great to see a book capturing the magical journey of Indian football being written. It is important that every aspect of Indian football reaches the readers, right from the time that the sport made its presence felt in India to the time when India has made its presence felt in the biggest stage of World football, the FIFA U-17 World Cup India 2017.

Today we are at a crucial juncture in the history of football in India and it's always nice to revisit the glorious past. I wish the book, *India's Football Dream* and its authors Mr Shantanu Gupta and Mr Nikhil Paramjit Sharma the very best and hope it serves as a tool to educate every Indian about the 'beautiful game' in our country.

Praful Patel, *President, All India Football Federation*

I feel a great sense of pride each time I pull on the India national team jersey. To represent India has been the greatest honour for me. Even when I was in Norway playing for Stabaek, I did believe I was indeed representing my country being the first Indian to play in the Europa Cup. It is important readers get to know the history of Indian football and the various stories related to it. Our current India national team is doing well and the U-17 World Cup brought the attention of the world to India. It's nice that the book aims to take the readers through this majestic journey.

Gurpreet Singh Sandhu, *India National Team Goalkeeper, First Indian to play in the UEFA Europa League*

Although I grew up in the UK, I have been very interested in the progression of football in India. I have never hidden my desire to play for the Indian National team and hopefully that will become a reality soon. *India's Football Dream* is a good reference point for anyone looking to understand the past and present of Indian football.

Daniel 'Danny' Tanveer Batth, *Wolverhampton Wolves*

Best wishes for the book by Nikhil and Shantanu. I am sure the book will serve as a good reminder to every reader why football in India has been, is, and will be a hugely popular sport across the length and breadth of the country. Thanks for putting together a comprehensive guide on Indian football that is sure to capture the reader's imagination.

Subrata Paul, *Indian National Team Goalkeeper, Legend of the game. Nicknamed 'Spiderman' by Indian football fans*

Our nation is passing through a dynamic and transient phase. It is entering a new era in its history wherein by 2022, more than half the population of this country will be only twenty-eight years of age making India one of the youngest countries in the world. I believe this new era will also see the country move from being largely a one sport nation to a Multi-Sport nation where football could emerge as the most popular sport in India in the next ten years. It remains to be seen if India will be a large consumer or market for International football or whether it will also emerge as a strong participant of the game and evolve a robust internal ecosystem of the beautiful game in the country.

I believe *India's Football Dream* has been written at an interesting junction just as Indian football enters its watershed period and I am sure that it will be an interesting read for all sports lovers in this country. I wish the book all the success it deserves and hope that it contributes in its own little way to the development and growth of a more sports and health conscious India.

Larsing 'Ming' Sawyan, *Vice President—All India Football Federation, Managing Director—Shillong Lajong Football Club*

INDIA'S FOOTBALL DREAM

INDIA'S FOOTBALL DREAM

SHANTANU GUPTA

NIKHIL PARAMJIT SHARMA

Los Angeles | London | New Delhi
Singapore | Washington DC | Melbourne

Copyright © Shantanu Gupta and Nikhil Paramjit Sharma, 2019

All rights reserved. No part of this book may be reproduced or utilised in any form or by any means, electronic or mechanical, including photocopying, recording, or by any information storage or retrieval system, without permission in writing from the publisher.

First published in 2019 by

SAGE Publications India Pvt Ltd
B1/I-1 Mohan Cooperative Industrial Area
Mathura Road, New Delhi 110 044, India
www.sagepub.in

Vitasta Publishing Pvt Ltd
2/15 Ansari Road, Daryaganj
Delhi 110002
www.vitastapublishing.com

SAGE Publications Inc
2455 Teller Road
Thousand Oaks, California 91320, USA

SAGE Publications Ltd
1 Oliver's Yard, 55 City Road
London EC1Y 1SP, United Kingdom

SAGE Publications Asia-Pacific Pte Ltd
18 Cross Street #10-10/11/12
China Square Central
Singapore 048423

Published by Vivek Mehra for SAGE Publications India Pvt Ltd, typeset in 10.5/13.5 pt Bembo by Fidus Design Pvt Ltd, Chandigarh.

Library of Congress Cataloging-in-Publication Data Available

ISBN: 978-93-532-8305-6 (PB)

SAGE Vitasta Team: Veena Batra, Namarita Kathait, Alekha Chandra Jena and Ritu Chopra

DEDICATION

Shantanu Gupta
Dedicating this book to my wife Swetha, son Abhiram and my newborn baby girl Nakshatra.

Nikhil Paramjit Sharma
Would like to dedicate this book to my parents Paramjit and Ragini, wife Urvashi, brother Karan and my friend and mentor, Sunny. Also would like to dedicate it to two close friends who unfortunately aren't with us anymore, Rishish and Rohan.

Thank you for choosing a SAGE product!
If you have any comment, observation or feedback,
I would like to personally hear from you.

Please write to me at **contactceo@sagepub.in**

Vivek Mehra, Managing Director and CEO, SAGE India.

Bulk Sales

SAGE India offers special discounts
for purchase of books in bulk.
We also make available special imprints
and excerpts from our books on demand.

For orders and enquiries, write to us at

Marketing Department
SAGE Publications India Pvt Ltd
B1/I-1, Mohan Cooperative Industrial Area
Mathura Road, Post Bag 7
New Delhi 110044, India

E-mail us at **marketing@sagepub.in**

Subscribe to our mailing list
Write to **marketing@sagepub.in**

This book is also available as an e-book.

CONTENTS

Foreword by Sunil Chhetri	ix
Preface	xiii
Acknowledgements	xvii
Dribbling through Football	1
History of Football in India	29
Regional Growth of Football	49
Football Clubs of India	79
Indian Leagues and Tournaments	111
Indian Super League	133
Indian National Team	147
AIFF and Other Federations	167
Initiatives to Boost the Game	175
FIFA Under-17 Football World Cup	185
About the Authors	217

FOREWORD

Football, it wouldn't be wrong to say, is in my blood. Both my parents played football with my father having played for the Indian army. Football occupies the place closest to my heart and it wouldn't be an understatement to say nothing else comes as close. As a young boy, playing football at various army campus grounds across the country, I did dream about wearing the blue of India some day but could never imagine what the sport would eventually bring to my life. Indian football has given me everything that I could ever dream of. I consider myself fortunate and blessed that I could serve my country in the way I have been able to. The country has seen many legends pull on the blue jersey and I consider myself lucky to have played alongside a few of them. Each time I wear the Indian colours now, I feel the sense of responsibility I have towards the fans and the joy my teammates and I can bring to our countrymen. I have now played 100 plus games for India having scored more than 60 goals. I have won the I-League four times along with numerous other trophies including the honour of being awarded the Arjuna Award by the Government of India in 2011; yet the zeal, the hunger and enthusiasm to do the best for football in India remains the same as it was when I first started out.

As a young boy, starting out in the football world in Delhi, my ambition was to go on and carve a name for myself in the footballing world and it has been a privilege to play for some of the top clubs across the length and breadth of India. I have played for three clubs in Kolkata—Mohun Bagan, East Bengal and United SC and can tell you that the fervour, excitement and passion that West Bengal has for the sport is infectious. You cannot be a Bengali and not know your football. Football fans in Bengal are extremely knowledgeable and have great respect for footballers. I have played and won the I-League with Dempo & Churchill Brothers in Goa and again the spark that football ignites in the minds of young Goan players and fans is unmatchable. Five years back I decided to venture out in what I would call a start-up in footballing sense. Despite offers from many I-League clubs in 2013, I decided to join what was then a new club coming up in Bengaluru. Bengaluru FC, a new entrant formed by JSW, was a fresh lease of life to the I-League and the way every one at this club has gone about their work of revolutionizing the way football is run in the country has left me extremely proud to have been chosen to be a part of this project.

Indian Super League was born in the year 2014 and while I did miss being a part of this great spectacle the first season, to be able to play for Mumbai City the next two seasons gave me great joy. I am back here in Bengaluru having committed my future to BFC as we started our life in the Indian Super League after four years in the I-League where we won the I-League title twice and Federation Cup an equal number of times. An appearance in the AFC Cup Finals against Iraq's Air Force club also remains a high point for me during that period. Both the I-League and ISL have contributed immensely to the development of Indian football in the past decade or so. The huge disappointment of losing the Indian Super League Finals in 2017/18 was marginally eased by the Hero Super Cup Win.

I have also been fortunate to have gotten chances to play in Europe and in America with Sporting Club De Portugal and Kansas City. It was a great learning experience for me to compare myself with absolutely the best talent in the world and also realise what it took to be a top football player. I wish the opportunity had come to me sooner when I was a teenager. However, the zeal to improve and get better stays with me. I believe it is my obligation to share the knowledge I have gained through various experiences in my playing career with younger players so they are better prepared to take on the challenges that await them. The AIFF and various other organisations attached to Indian football have done a great job in the past to focus on grassroots football development and that's one area we cannot neglect. Only once the foundation of the building is strong does the entire building have a chance of being a robust structure.

From the time I made my Senior National Team debut against Pakistan in 2005 till date, the joy of wearing the Indian jersey remains. I have enjoyed every game that I have played so far for India and while there have been defeats along the way that bogged us down, the joy of winning games and trophies for the country outweighs them all. Qualifying and playing the 2011 AFC Asian Cup remains one of my most memorable moments, where we qualified after a gap of twenty-four years. The 2007, 2009 and 2012 Nehru Cup wins for India and the 2008 Asian Challenge Cup were memorable moments of my career. Scoring goals and helping India win matches has been the greatest personal satisfaction for me. Captaining the side is an honour I am privileged to have. I wish I am able to continue contributing to Indian football on the pitch for as long as I can and as we head to 2019 AFC Asia Cup I hope the Indian team writes another golden chapter in its illustrious history.

This book as the title suggests is aimed at taking the reader through a journey of Indian football. Right from the origin of the sport the world across to how the game came to India. It talks about how various regions took to the sport and what clubs have played their part in making this sport popular. Unlike any other sport, clubs are a lifeline for the sport of football. The world across, clubs such as Manchester United, Barcelona, Bayern Munich, Juventus, Santos are the ones that have made the sport as popular if not more than the country teams such as Brazil, Italy, Germany and others. India has a great history of some fine clubs too. India has also some of the oldest football tournaments like the Federation Cup, the Durand Cup and Rovers Cup. These tournaments, along with the I-League and Indian Super League, give the clubs a place to compete. The readers will find interesting information about these tournaments and leagues in the book. I am glad the book covers the exploits of the Indian National Team which includes some of the national team stars that I looked up to while growing up. Finally, it talks extensively about an event which put India firmly on the world map as a footballing country; the FIFA U-17 World Cup. Sometimes I wish I was still an U-17 player and was eligible to play in the World Cup. Anyway, it was a wonderful event and the kind of football passion we saw all across India bodes well for the future of the game. We now have a first-hand account of where we are and what we have to do as a country to get to the top of the footballing charts.

I have known Nikhil for quite some time having first met him in Delhi a few years back. I wish Shantanu and him the very best for this endeavour of theirs and hope *India's Football Dream* achieves the objective it set out for—to tell the unique story of Indian football to millions of Indians and other football fans across the world.

—**Sunil Chhetri**
Captain, Indian Football Team

PREFACE

The year 2017 was a historic year for Indian football in many ways. India hosted the FIFA Under-17 World Cup in the month of October 2017. The Indian national team qualified for the 2019 Asia Cup to be held in Qatar while Aizawl FC scripted a fairytale I-League win. Atletico de Kolkata won their second Indian Super League title in what was only the third season for the ISL. Across the length and breadth of the country, football has slowly but surely made its way to becoming a popular sport. It has regained some of its lost sheen from earlier times when the country was doing well in the international arena and the sport was very actively played at the grassroots level across the country.

The journey for this book began with our meeting at a football match in July 2016 which was followed by an extensive discussion session about football in India at Shantanu's office. Shantanu has worked extensively in the development and social sector across the length and breadth of the country and had a keen interest in how football served as a key tool in the developmental aspect of not just the sport but society overall. Nikhil has now been working in the sports sphere for almost a decade with football occupying a major part of that work. As a sports management professional whose span of work includes heading a sports management group with operations in India, being a director on board an I-League team and a grassroots development club to leading the inception of an Indian Super League side, Nikhil had very closely watched Indian football grow from a technical and commercial standpoint in the last few years. During one of these long conversations, we realised that a large part of the Indian football story had gone untold. As cricket continued its domination on the Indian sporting scene for almost three decades, football in India had taken a backseat, and until a few years back occupied lesser significance in the minds of sports lovers in the country. Shantanu was deep into research for another book at that point and the idea of putting together the story of Indian football had to wait until the start of 2017. In March we decided to put together what we called a beginner's guide to Indian football. It was important for us to introduce the past, present and future of the game in India to the sports lovers across the country and overseas.

The history of football in India is an illustrious one with each one of the key players occupying an illustrious place in the history books. To put together so many of these stories succinctly in one book seemed like a challenge in itself. We, along with our research team, very carefully collated the information. It was important to start the book by setting the background to the greatest sport in the world with something of the genesis of the sport of football itself. How the game started in its primitive form almost two centuries ago and how it spread across the world; it's entry into India through the British troops that were deployed here and how it moved across the country. The sport inevitably found favour with a few specific regions and while it continued to be popular across the country, certain bastions were formed where it was much more popular.

Clubs are a lifeline for football. The world over, club football keeps the fans glued to the sport and India has seen extremely strong brands come up over the last century and a half. It was imperative to highlight all these clubs across India and the role they played in making football an immensely popular sport. These clubs have traditionally played in tournaments and India has been home to some of the oldest tournaments in world football. The Federation

Cup and the Durand Cup along with the Rovers Cup occupy a unique place in the world football history books and they kept the interest in football alive long before pan India league football took precedence. The Calcutta Football League has been in existence since almost the introduction of football in India and hence finds mention time and again in the book. India's revival in world football or rather at an international level happened partly as a result of putting together a strong nationwide league which enabled talented Indian players to play year long. The National Football League along with the I-League moved the technical side of Indian football forward but, over a period of time, the fan interest had started dwindling a wee bit. That's where the Indian Super League gave a new lease of life to the stadium going football audience. Sparked by the tie-up between All India Football Federation and Reliance-IMG, the ISL was first introduced as an IPL of football. Now the league is veering towards traditional long season format. The Indian national team features in the book as a chapter taking the readers back to the pre-independence days. The chapter also talks about all the great players that the national team has featured. All Indian Football Federation is the governing body of the sport in India and its formation is an interesting story in itself. There have been some notable efforts in 'football for a cause' sector and we felt it was important to highlight these. Finally, the FIFA Under-17 World Cup that took place in October of 2017 has been the cynosure of all eyes and putting an event of this magnitude together has firmly entrenched India in the global football scenario.

This book aspires to speak for, and on behalf of, the sport of football in India which has had an illustrious past and is now primed to become one of the most important social tools in our country.

ACKNOWLEDGEMENTS

This has been a remarkable journey of understanding and knowing far more about football in India than we could have ever without the intent to put this project together. It wasn't the easiest but was definitely thoroughly enjoyable. It would not have been possible without our support of each other and of those who came together to help us put this piece together.

Sunil Chhetri was gracious enough to write the foreword for us. It's a huge honour for us to have the Indian national team captain writing the foreword for this book and we can't thank him enough. Sonu Lamba from Four Flags helped us put this together with Sunil. We've received encouraging words and good wishes from AIFF President Mr Praful Patel and AIFF Vice President Mr Larsing Ming Sawyan and we would like to thank them for their support. Subrata Paul and Gurpreet Singh Sandhu, both gave us their messages and Danny Batth penned his thoughts on the book as well. Not without reason are you guys the champions that you are. Media teams and managers at almost all clubs were gracious and helpful. Special thanks to Nilanjan Datta, Shoubhik Mukhopadhyay and AIFF media team; Kunaal Majgaonkar and the Bengaluru FC media team; and Janice Lynrah and Shillong Lajong media team for making a huge chunk of photographs available to us in a short period of time. A lot of content in the book has been inspired by conversations with so many passionate professionals working in the footballing ecosystem in India. Ashish Shah (Delhi Dynamos), Ranjit Bajaj

(Minerva Punjab), Shaji Prabhakaran (Delhi Soccer Association), Sunando Dhar and his I-League team (AIFF), Joy Bhattacharya, Roma Khanna, Javier Ceppi and Arup Soans (LOC—FIFA U-17 World Cup), Varun Achreja (Football Solutions), Indranil Das Blah and Watson Fernandes (Mumbai City), Chirag Tanna, Rochak Langer, G Srinivasan, Leeladhar Singh, Hoshedar Gundevia, Vivan Patel and Yash Patel from Reliance-IMG combine, Henry Menezes (WIFA), Atul Bagdamia (Mumbai FC), Gaurav Modwel and Tejas Goradia (FC Pune City), Neel Shah (formerly with DSK Shivajians), Victor Fernandes (Sporting Club de Goa), Raj Gomes and Adlear D'Cruz (Salgaocar SC), Sujay Sharma (ATK), Mandar Tamhane (Bengaluru FC), Varun Tripuraneni (Kerala Blasters), Rohit Ramesh (Chennai City FC), Bino George and Praveen VC (Gokulam Kerala), Yogesh Maurya (Fateh Hyderabad), Debashish Dutta, Imran Khan and Sanjoy Ghosh (Mohun Bagan), Habamutlang Lyngdoh and Andrew Suting (Shillong Lajong) and Luiz Greco (International Director Atletico Paranaense).

We have been greatly inspired and learnt a great deal from various coaches who have tirelessly served the sport in India. It's important to mention some who inspired us to write this book— Savio Medeira, Richard Hood, Rob Baan, Scott O'Donnell, Derrick Pereira, Pradhyum Reddy and Thangboi Singto.

The biggest stars of the sport of football are the players and there are numerous footballers who have inspired us through this journey. Thank you so much for being the shining stars of football in India and for serving the sport with such dedication.

Our research team of Abhijit Bharali, Arkodeepto Mukherjee and Swapnaneel Parasar who enabled us to gather so much material.

Finally, our respective families and friends who've had to bear the brunt of our writing spells and moods. Hopefully, we've managed to put together something that will be informative and will stir up a great sense of belonging and pride towards football in India.

CHAPTER 1
DRIBBLING THROUGH FOOTBALL

Football—'The Beautiful Game', a term[1] coined by television presenter and football commentator Stuart Hall in 1958 while being awed by Manchester City's Peter Doherty, was perhaps the only sport that drew so many people together for a common cause. There was a reason why the sport of football was called 'The Beautiful Game' in popular culture. Footballers were worshipped like demi-gods—the likes of Pele and Diego Maradona were eternal symbols of that, while the more modern Lionel Messi and Cristiano Ronaldo are their present-day representations.

Football was brought to India by British soldiers, in the late nineteenth century, when they accidently carried it in their kit-bags.[2] Since then, the football culture has seen a rise, the most visible manifestation of which was the country hosting the Fédération Internationale de Football Association[3] (FIFA) Under-17 World Cup in October 2017.

The FIFA Under-17 World Cup marked the first time India had staged a global football tournament and its national team had participated in it. This book is an attempt to align the 1.34 billion and counting population[4] of India towards the beautiful game, with the biggest football event that the country had hosted as a backdrop. Football's following in India has always been there and is now coming to the fore in many ways. To understand where it stems from let us first dive into the past, to where the game can be retraced to its first steps, to what it is today.

★

The British were the first to formally introduce football to the world in the late nineteenth century, although the sport of kicking

---

[1] https://www.theguardian.com/football/2003/may/02/newsstory.sport11
[2] *Nation at Play: History of Sport in India*, Ronojoy Sen
[3] www.fifa.com/
[4] http://www.worldometers.info/world-population/india-population/

a ball was prevalent as early as the second and third centuries BC in China.[5] Rugby and football were fairly similar when the classification of the sport started with quite a lot of rules used interchangeably. Ultimately, the two sports continued to evolve and are today played as two distinct sports.

Soccer is an alternate name for football in countries like US, Canada, Australia and a few others. There is an interesting theory behind the word 'soccer'. The coining of the word 'soccer' reportedly traces its history as a distinguishing factor between Association Football and Rugby Football. While Association Football in slang was called 'Assoca' which further developed into soccer, Rugby Football came to be known as 'Rugga'. Though Rugby returned to its original name fairly soon, Assoca travelled far and wide into the Americas with students travelling from Britain. Back home when people had reverted to 'football', 'soccer' stuck around in the US, Canada and Australia as an alternative name.

With the formation of the English Football Association (FA) in 1863, football, or Association Football as it was formally known, became coded into different sets of rules and protocols that are in use even today. The concept of handling the ball was banned for outfielders, while rough tackling or hacking as it was called was outlawed and the duration of a football match was set at ninety minutes. Football gradually cleaned up and was seen as a completely different entity from Rugby, its erstwhile partner. The sport began to be played competitively, with football clubs representing local communities sprouting everywhere, allowing youngsters to practise the sport, starting from Great Britain.

Among the first football clubs of modern design was Sheffield FC, which is still the oldest surviving football club, founded in 1857. Before Sheffield FC, however, there was Cambridge University FC, which was founded in 1856.[6] It was Cambridge that saw the drafting

---

[5] http://www.fifa.com/about-fifa/who-we-are/the-game/index.html
[6] http://www.bbc.co.uk/cambridgeshire/content/articles/2006/06/09/cambridge_football_rules_parkers_piece_feature.shtml

of the 'Cambridge Rules'—the first codes of how the game of football should be played. An FA committee member[7] has an interesting take on the Sheffield-Cambridge debate, '... There's room for both clubs in the record books; Cambridge University for the rules and Sheffield as the world's first true football club!'

That being said, modern, professional football only came into being in the early twentieth century. Sheffield FC's birth in 1857 was followed by the emergence of Hallam FC, Cray Wanderers, Worksop Town and Notts County in the subsequent years. By 1862, fifteen clubs were dotted in the Sheffield region only. While Sheffield FC remains the first true football club, Notts County founded in 1862, is the oldest fully professional football club. Incidentally, Sheffield FC, in its colourful history, has also played in India as recently as 2010, when it squared off to the big three of Kolkata football—Mohun Bagan, East Bengal and Mohammedan Sporting—in an invitational tournament.

The big three of Kolkata football also happened to be among the oldest football clubs in India. As India had been under British rule since 1858, football too began to be part of the Indian psyche, with the British capital city of Calcutta (now Kolkata) being the birthplace of football in India. Mohun Bagan was among the first Indian clubs to be formed,[8] along with Town Club, Kumartuli Institute and Aryan Club. Bagan was founded in 1889, whereas the other three were established between 1884 and 1886. Mohammedan Sporting began to exist in 1891, after the coming together of the sizeable Muslim community of Bengal.[9] One other member of the big three—East Bengal—came into being later in 1920, when a section of the Jorabagan Club hierarchy broke away and founded

---

[7] http://www.bbc.co.uk/cambridgeshire/content/articles/2006/06/09/cambridge_football_rules_parkers_piece_feature.shtml
[8] https://www.telegraphindia.com/1140710/jsp/opinion/story_18596803.jsp
[9] http://www.thehardtackle.com/2011/legends-of-indian-football-mohammedan-sporting-in-1930s/

Spectators stand on bicycles to catch glimpse of Kolkata League

a new football club, thereby starting a deep-rooted Indian football rivalry that is prominent even today.

Back to England and speaking of rivalries, Sheffield FC's local rivalry with Hallam FC is the oldest derby in world football, another significant part of the sport's cultural appeal. Derby matches are games between local rivals, and over the years, derbies have assumed great importance, so much so, that the 'El Clasico' rivalry between Real Madrid and Barcelona in Spain has become the very definition of football in Spain,[10] much as the Kolkata rivalry is the overarching theme of football in Bengal. 'El Clasico' has evolved over the years and has now become almost mythical with Ronaldo and Messi being the chief protagonists—just like the sport of football itself.

The evolution of football over its more than 150 years of existence is interesting, with Great Britain being widely accepted as the founding father of the sport as we now know. Football, in the Victorian era, was headlined by representative teams of British infantry that played across the globe, including India, and who introduced the sport to newer places. The English 'Mister' is used in Latin American and Iberian countries to address coaches

---

[10] *Fear and Loathing in La Liga*, Sid Lowe

and managers, a symbol of how different football cultures have been influenced by the British. Ironically, the British game has been outgrown by other cultures in Western countries, the seeds of which were sown by the British themselves. An apt description of the contribution of the British can be found on the cover of Rory Smith's book, *Mister*,[11] which reads, 'The men who taught the world how to beat England at their own game.' Furthermore, the British were at the forefront of how the dynamics of football has changed over the years.

While coding of the laws of football was the sport's first target when it took shape in the late 1880s, the early-to-mid-twentieth century saw a rise in the analytical perceptions of football. As the game became popular, a tactical view—based on individual analysis of players and teams—became pronounced, as has been suggested by the well-documented Herbert Chapman's W-M formation. As a result, more and more amateur football clubs turned professional after figuring out how popular the sport was with the masses.

Germany, in particular, is a fine case in point.

Germany, the four-time FIFA World Cup champions, had been severely affected by the two World Wars in the twentieth century and hence, had a skeptical view of the sport as a profession. Football clubs in Germany had never solely been football clubs. According to Uli Hesse in his book, *Tor*, 'They [German football clubs] are, without exception, multisport associations which offer their members a variety of athletic activities.' Gymnastics and physical activities were common at German clubs, where the English model of earning money through playing sports was looked down upon. Considering that, German football (West and East combined) has come a long way in becoming what has now turned into a blueprint across the world, after the German national team's World Cup win in 2014.

---

[11] *Mister*, Rory Smith

The German Bundesliga is presently one of the most popular football leagues in the world, but its birth year of 1963 means that it is a relatively young league. West German football turned fully professional only after their 1954 World Cup-winning Coach Sepp Herberger, lobbied[12] relentlessly with the German Football Association (DFB) for a national league instead of the traditional regional leagues which would, in a way, allow footballers to pursue the sport professionally. Herberger had an upper hand, having restored West Germany's prestige somewhat after the trauma of the World Wars by surprisingly winning the 1954 World Cup. His wishes were met when West German football walked away from the regional league system and formed a national league. With West German football having turned fully professional with the advent of the Bundesliga, football across the world also turned professional at large. West Germany was among the last big football nations to champion the notion of football as a profession.

Gradually, football moved away from its sport-only definition. It became a brand, with fiercely contested continental competitions like the European Cup widely followed, and its marketability was high because of its connection with the people—mostly the match-going public.

As a footnote, the Bundesliga also has a connection with Indian football, which started in the mid-2000s when the DFB and the All India Football Federation (AIFF) agreed to a partnership. India has since then entertained several German clubs—Bayern Munich, Hoffenheim, Borussia Dortmund—who came to the country either with players or with officials.

★

Before the wildly popular European Cup (now known as the Champions League) which was established in 1955, the British gave the world the idea of cup competitions. The Football Association

---

[12] *Tor*, Uli Hesse

Challenge Cup (FA Cup), the oldest football cup competition in the world, started in 1871 with Wanderers FC winning the first title. The FA Cup, retooled in the 1888–89 season when qualifying rounds were introduced, still runs strong, with Arsenal having won the most recent edition in 2017. The FA Cup was followed by the commencement of various national cup competitions across the world. Scotland and Wales followed suit soon after and football began to be competitively played across the United Kingdom in the late nineteenth century.

The oldest national football league, the Argentina Primera Division, started in 1891 and soon after, India entered the football history books with the Durand Cup and the IFA Shield[13]—the two oldest competitions in the country. The concept of full-fledged league football spread from Argentina across the world, so much so, that almost every FIFA-recognised member association in the world now has domestic leagues.

The IFA was exclusive only to the British to begin with, with no Indians allowed into the body until 1920. Somnath Sengupta, an Indian football writer, penned, 'IFA Shield was started in 1893, making it the fourth oldest football competition in history. Curiously, Indians were not allowed to join in the Indian Football Federation till the 1920s. IFA consisted of high-ranking British army officials while football tournaments usually included British regiment teams,' suggesting that the IFA Shield was a rarefied space reserved for the ruling British. British hegemony in the IFA Shield was broken memorably by the Mohun Bagan team of 1911 that beat the East Yorkshire Regiment 2-1 in the final—becoming the first Indian football team to defeat an English team and win the IFA Shield. The goalscorers of that match, Shibdas Bhaduri and Abhilash Ghosh, have since become legends of the Indian game, and on 15th May 2017, the former's senior-most surviving kin, Gouri Bhaduri, was presented with the first ticket of

---

[13] http://www.thehardtackle.com/2011/the-glorious-history-of-ifa-shield/

the FIFA Under-17 World Cup, commemorating an occasion that changed Indian football forever.

However, before Bagan's epic triumph, a team from Sovabazar toppled a British team representing the East Surrey Regiment in 1892, but that achievement as the first Indian win over the British in football has since been a footnote in history. The fact is that five years before the advent of the IFA Shield, the oldest football tournament in India started—the Durand Cup. It was the brainchild of former Indian foreign secretary Mortimer Durand and initially featured teams representing different British and Indian cavalry units. Over the course of history, both the IFA Shield and the Durand Cup have undergone changes; the former is now contested by Under-19 teams of Indian clubs, while the latter witnesses a proliferation of professional football clubs apart from the Indian Armed Forces' teams.

Besides the cup competitions that featured club teams or represented organisations like the FA Cup and the IFA Shield, there were also tournaments between national teams. This concept was developed well after the inception of the FA Cup or the Durand Cup, with the Copa America—an international tournament featuring countries from Latin America, kicking off for the first time in 1916. In the process, it became the first major international tournament, featuring Confederación Sudamericana de Fútbol (CONMEBOL) nations. Fourteen years later, the FIFA World Cup took shape, and in the subsequent years other confederations followed Copa America's lead and came up with continental tournaments. Although international football had been part of the Summer Olympic Games since 1900, its prestige has dwindled with time, leading to the competition in its current state being effectively an Under-23 event that takes place every four years.

★

Wherever the British moved they took the game with them. Little did they imagine that a fire fuelled by one of their own, a Scottish man named Thomas Donohoe would ultimately give birth to possibly the greatest football nation in the world. Thomas Donohoe organised the first recognised football match in 1894 in Rio, Brazil, and his contribution to the sport has been rewarded with a statue in the textile factory he organised the match in.[14] The games Donohoe was popular for playing reportedly featured six players vs six players—so the modern day concept of Futsal or small sided games is not so modern after all.[15]

What's football without some rivalry though, and the great Scotsman had a rival too—he was from Sao Paulo. Charles Miller was born to a Scottish railway engineer and was sent to pursue his education in Southampton FC. An athletic Charles soon took to football and was in no time playing for 'The Saints' Southampton FC. He played a few games for Corinthians as well. His return to Brazil featured two footballs and a book containing thirteen rules of football. On 14 April 1985, British workers of Sao Paolo Railway Company took on a team from the Gas Company in a match that was widely considered the first recognised football match in Brazil. This was till the Donohoe story gained steam and Sao Paolo was left a tad disappointed that the Brazilian football story did not start from there. There has been a lot to cheer for in Brazil since then, as they have won almost every title on the offering in World football, winning the World Cup five times— the most by any nation. Olympic titles and Copa America titles have not stayed away from them either. Football to Brazil is what cricket is to Indians. They are made for each other.

The other Latin American countries have not stayed too far away. In fact, Brazil's neighbour, Argentina, was the first to open its arms to 'The Beautiful Game'. As early as May 1867, two Englishmen—Thomas and James Hogg—organised a meeting in

---

[14] http://www.dailyrecord.co.uk/news/uk-world-news/glaswegian-who-took-football-brazil-3544338
[15] http://grassroots.fifa.com/en/for-kids/small-sided-games.html

Buenos Aires where the first football club—Buenos Aires Football Club—was born. Incidentally, the Buenos Aires Cricket Club gave their football counterparts permission to use their ground Parquetres De Febrero. 20 June 1967 saw its first game being played there. The European community took football far and wide as the Dutch influenced football in Paraguay. The United States and Canada were not left behind with the Europeans there taking to the sport. In 1929, Costa Rica was one of the first to align itself to FIFA which was formed in 1904. Mexico was up next. The sport grew rapidly in Southern America as Brazil and Argentina took a fancy to the sport, which had replaced traditional sports in the country as the number one sport of choice.

Asia remained fairly untouched by the magic of football, or rather did not see the rapid growth in the sport at the same pace as some of its continental colleagues. The Asian Football Confederation (AFC) which was formed only in 1954 followed suit first with the Asian Cup's formation in 1957. Africa, another continent that saw colonisation, was highly influenced by the sport, while countries such as South Africa, Egypt and Algeria saw people taking to the sport as early as the end of nineteenth century. The sport has since then taken a huge leap and is now considered to be the most followed sport across the entire continent, with young African players garnering the attention of everyone in the footballing world.

Speaking of competitions, Africa's Cup of Nations was launched only in 1958. The Union of European Football Associations (UEFA) started the European Championship in 1960, while the Confederation of North, Central America and Caribbean Association Football (CONCACAF) Gold Cup joined the party late in 1991. Oceania's Nations Cup first came about in 1973, but formally started only in 1996.

India has only participated in the AFC Asian Cup thrice, the last of which was in 2011. India's football history is littered with its impressive displays in the Olympic Games and the Asian Games, and regional international tournaments. The Indian national team's international honours include gold medals at the Asian Games in 1951 and 1962, three Nehru Cup wins, one AFC Challenge Cup and six SAFF Championships—none of them are FIFA-handled tournaments. All these competitions, cups and leagues, national and international, form the backbone of the football world. India, too, is part of this global race that continues to grow with time, but fighting for the World Cup remains the ultimate dream of the nation.

★

The FIFA World Cup is the biggest football spectacle on earth. The quadrennial event has been around since 1930, with far fewer teams participating in the World Cup's earlier editions than today. Stephen Dobson and John Goddard put the World Cup's magnitude into perspective in their book, *The Economics of Football*, 'The World Cup is the most widely viewed sporting event in the world; the estimated cumulative television audience for the 2006 World Cup in Germany was 26.2 billion, an average of 409 million viewers per match.'[16] The World Cup is a reflection of how the world of football has changed. Upon its inception in 1928 by Frenchman Jules Rimet, the FIFA president at that time, the global event's inaugural edition in 1930 hosted thirteen contestants. In 2026, the World Cup will see forty-eight participating nations,[17] proving just how the world of football has expanded at an exponential rate in all these years. The most successful nation in the World Cup is Brazil, laying its hands on the holy grail a record of five times. While Brazil's South American counterparts, Uruguay and Argentina, have each won the World Cup twice equalled by France who have won the World Cup in 1998 and 2018, European heavyweights, Germany and Italy, have proved more successful, each winning four times. England and Spain are

---

[16] https://en.wikipedia.org/wiki/FIFA_World_Cup#cite_note-3
[17] http://www.fifa.com/about-fifa/news/y=2017/m=1/news=fifa-council-unanimously-decides-on-expansion-of-the-fifa-world-cuptm--2863100.html

the other nations to have won the World Cup in its twenty-one-edition history.

Despite the growing affinity of the Indian population towards football, playing in a World Cup for the national team still remains a distant dream. India has never played in a World Cup, having spurned a lucky chance in 1950 when it qualified by default after Indonesia, Philippines and Burma pulled out because of logistical issues. Moreover, the World Cup's low priority in the eyes of the then All India Football Federation (AIFF) meant that India let its Brazil chance pass.[18] Contrasting versions of the events of 1950 state that Mohun Bagan's win over East Yorkshire Regiment in the 1911 IFA Shield playing barefooted, created an identity of Indian football. The subsequent generations of Indian footballers played on the same principles, and since India played football barefoot, the FIFA rules that forced teams to sport shoes came in its way and killed its World Cup dream. Indian football had since then faded into oblivion on the world stage until recently, with its millions of fans starved of a global event appearance for generations.

Governments, Federations, Clubs and various private initiatives in India have tried to improve football in India over the last decade or so. Most importantly, the advent of Indian Super League (ISL) has placed Indian football at the front end of football galleries the world over. In the last couple of years, the government is working closely with FIFA and AIFF for the development of football in India. As a result, India has phenomenally improved its ranking from 173 in March 2015 to being in the late 90s now. The FIFA U-17 World Cup held in October 2017 saw an Indian team play in a World Cup for the first time ever, and while it was only an age group World Cup the hype and euphoria surrounding the appearance of the Indians was justified.

★

---

[18] https://www.bloomberg.com/view/articles/2014-06-11/blame-india-s-world-cup-drought-on-the-shoes

Global football is a multilayered phenomenon. There is an obvious food chain wherein the biggest European clubs can spend the most amount of money in the sport, followed by the rest of Europe, USA, Asia, South America and so on. The English Premier League, rebranded in its current form in 1992, is now a behemoth of a product, attracting millions and millions of fans from across the globe to a unique offering, thereby bringing back far more than what is invested. Talking of food chains, in modern day football, clubs are generally hierarchically recognised based on their financial might rather than the trophies and shields they have won. The birth of super clubs like Barcelona and Bayern Munich has changed the very dimension of football today.

Some also feel that professional football clubs playing at the very top level are no longer mere football clubs with a strictly community-based essence. Old timers say that football clubs are now big businesses, as success off the pitch has become as integral as success on it. Star names are bought to enhance a club's standing as a global force. Sporting success alone is not enough anymore. The modern football fan is a fickle person, and clubs must work hard towards keeping him satisfied all the time, whether by winning football matches or by recruiting fancy players for big sums of money. This is one reason why we regularly witness English clubs making record transfers, and why modern football has discovered alternate definitions of success, so much so that a cheque book can be more valuable than a packed cabinet.

Because of all the money that is put in, the focus on returns is always under the scanner. At the truly global level, football clubs pursue various interests to make profits on millions of dollars in investments. They mostly rely on three sources for revenue generation—matchday revenue, commercial revenue and broadcasting revenue, but other forms of income generation are also being explored, judging by the increasing investment in the world's biggest clubs from Russia and countries in the Middle East and East Asia.

Matchday revenue is the income clubs generate via gate receipts and ticket sales. Since the capacity of football grounds is not a dynamic entity, football clubs can only do so much to increase their matchday revenue. One reason why we see elite clubs offer more hospitality tickets is to maximise the matchday revenue, which also depends on the geography and demography of the club. For example, in India, a football club in Kerala or West Bengal will make more matchday revenue because of their bigger football-loving population, whereas for a club in Madhya Pradesh, the matchday income will be much less owing to the relative lack of enthusiasm towards the sport in the region.

Commercial revenue is another important stream of money for football clubs. Clubs, as businesses, attract brands which, in turn, gain visibility on a larger scale because of football's mass appeal. The sponsors associate with football clubs at different levels—from the top level where brands become shirt sponsors to the lower rungs where a little footnote on the club's official website satisfies demands. Advertising deals with betting conglomerates[19] enhances the profile of the sponsors, leading to clubs making more money. It is very common these days to see football clubs selling naming rights of their home stadiums, an example of that being English Premier League club Arsenal's Emirates Stadium.

Lastly, the income from broadcasting plays a pivotal role in football clubs thriving in the current age of austerity.[20] The success of a football club is a continuous cycle, where glory on the pitch is rewarded with better opportunities off it, which in turn allow the club to use more money to sign the best footballers and managers, who tend to be more successful. The cycle keeps repeating until a point when decay sets in and a restart is required. Indian football

---

[19] http://www.fcbusiness.co.uk/news/article/newsitem=4993/title=how+football+clubs+source+their+revenue

[20] https://www.theguardian.com/football/2017/jul/14/kyle-walker-manchester-city-madness-premier-league

is on the path to formulate a structural change to align itself with global football.

★

An informal definition of a super club would be a club that is hugely successful on the pitch and wins silverware consistently while also boasting a fan base that stretches from one corner of the globe to another. In short, super clubs are the best run businesses in football. Only in the recent past has the rise of super clubs been more prominent. The Barcelona team under Pep Guardiola changed the way football was seen and played, and it won trophies relentlessly as well—winning six of them in 2009 alone. Jupp Heynckes' Bayern Munich swept all the trophies of 2012–13 season, breaking records and signalling itself as part of the increasingly exclusive circle of super clubs. The likes of Real Madrid, Juventus, Paris Saint-Germain and Manchester United also fall under the same category—clubs who are rarely affected by disastrous results on the pitch because their brand value is so strong. The Champions League regularly has winners from the small clique of super clubs, and domestic leagues have become increasingly predictable due to the dominance of the super clubs.

Football historian Jonathan Wilson noted in 2013,[21] 'For the biggest clubs, nationality, although not irrelevant, is a minor issue. What has developed rather is a small group of super clubs who transcend nationality, and because they're based in only four countries (arguably five if Paris Saint-Germain establish themselves), inevitably those sides occasionally meet in the final [of the Champions League].'

It can be argued that the advent of super clubs in the world football has heavily distorted the player transfer market. Whether it was for good or bad is open for debate, but footballers now make

---

[21] https://www.theguardian.com/football/blog/2013/may/21/champions-league-super-clubs

more money than ever before, from unprecedented avenues as well. Inflation in the football transfer market is different from standard inflation, in that it runs faster. Since the Premier League's inception in 1992, there has been more than a 1,000 per cent inflation in football.[22] If you consider all-time Premier League top scorer Alan Shearer as a case study, his 3.3-million-pound move from Southampton to Blackburn Rovers in 1992 would now be worth more than 40 million pounds in value. Football is always changing, but the emergence of super clubs has triggered a major shift, both in terms of football's popularity and the money that is flowing in, in the sport. Super clubs regularly have turnovers well over 500 million dollars, with the current top-earning football club Manchester United recording[23] more than 600 million dollars in turnovers in 2016. As the line between football and finance gets increasingly blurred, the downsides also become more apparent.

One big instance of that is the recent occurrence of the matter related to financial irregularities[24] that led to the downfall of Joseph S Blatter as the FIFA president in 2015 after a seventeen-year tenure, shaking the very foundations of FIFA. As the governing body of world football, FIFA works towards the betterment and development of the sport at all levels. That said, the current state of FIFA bears little resemblance to what transpired more than hundred years ago.

★

With 211 members, as of September 2018, FIFA now has more members than the United Nations. World across, the sport of football is governed by FIFA (Fédération Internationale de

---

[22] https://sports.vice.com/en_uk/article/gv7a3m/football-inflation-and-the-transfer-window
[23] https://www2.deloitte.com/content/dam/Deloitte/uk/Documents/sports-business-group/deloitte-uk-sport-football-money-league-2017.pdf
[24] https://www.theguardian.com/football/2015/dec/21/sepp-blatter-michel-platini-banned-from-football-fifa

Football Association), a private association which describes itself as an international governing body of association football, futsal and beach soccer.[25] FIFA is an association governed by Swiss law, founded in 1904 and based in Zurich. FIFA is responsible for the organisation of football's major international tournaments, notably the World Cup which commenced in 1930 and the Women's World Cup which commenced in 1991. FIFA was founded in 1904 to oversee international competition among the national associations of Belgium, Denmark, France, Germany, the Netherlands, Spain, Sweden and Switzerland.

FIFA's goal, enshrined in its Statutes, is the constant improvement of football.[26] Just to put in perspective as to how massive that number of 211 member nations is, we just need to have a look at the number of member nations currently with the United Nations which today stands at 193.[27] Not without a reason do football fans call the sport 'more than a religion'.

That essentially is the stamp on the popularity that the sport enjoys across every part of the world. Each one of the FIFA member nations should also be part of one of the six regional continental confederations associated with FIFA—Africa, Asia, Europe, North and Central America and the Caribbean, Oceania, and South America. India is a member of the Asian Football Confederation (AFC).

FIFA was founded in May 1904[28] when seven men—Robert Guérin and André Espir (France), Louis Muhlinghaus and Max Kahn (Belgium), Ludvig Sylow (Denmark), Carl Anton Wilhelm Hirschman (Netherlands), Victor E Schneider (Switzerland)—convened at the Union des Sociétés Française de Sports Athlétiques (USFSA) headquarters in Paris. Throughout, over 110 years of

---

[25] https://en.wikipedia.org/wiki/FIFA
[26] http://www.fifa.com/about-fifa/who-we-are/index.html
[27] http://www.un.org/en/member-states/
[28] http://www.fifa.com/about-fifa/who-we-are/history/index.html

its existence, FIFA has gone through myriad ups and downs, but it has never ceased to work, be it in the middle of the two World Wars or during the countless calamitous moments that have afflicted the world. FIFA has survived even the wildest of storms and its custodian in the present day is Swiss-Italian lawyer, Gianni Infantino.

FIFA's early days were without football's founding association, the English FA. Guerin became the first FIFA president in 1904, and it was his haste to establish FIFA that led to the non-participation of the British football associations as founding members of the governing body. However, it was the English FA's rulebook which FIFA first incorporated into its Statutes which laid down the regulations for football as an international game. A year later, in 1905, FIFA finally succeeded in persuading the English FA to join, and with that came the other British member associations—Scotland, Wales and Ireland—to FIFA's fold. The British influence in FIFA increased, leading to more uniformity in the implementation of the guidelines of the game, but French was established as FIFA's official language to salute the federation's birthplace. It was only in 1909 that FIFA entertained members from outside Europe, with South Africa, Argentina, Chile and the United States becoming FIFA members in the first-wave of non-European influx.

However, the breakout of the First World War brought about the disintegration of FIFA. In the aftermath of war, the British members pulled out, leaving the then chairman Jules Rimet with only twenty nations under FIFA's wing. In a bid to resurrect football and FIFA's standing, Rimet brought the Olympic football tournament under FIFA's umbrella, which was one of the first steps to the rise of football as a global sport. The hugely popular Olympic football tournament's success finally paved the way for the inception of the FIFA World Cup, which formally opened in 1930—thirty years after football made its Olympics debut. Throughout the years, FIFA has upheld the notion of football as a global sport and as of now, football is among the most widely played sports in the world with over 200 countries currently affiliated to FIFA.[29] Not only does FIFA promote football across the world, but it is also involved in numerous initiatives that maintain the essence of football as a community sport and how it can have an impact on different societies and cultures around the world. Its projects like 'Football for Hope' and 'Football for the Planet' have been steps towards ensuring that the world becomes a better place with the help of football, while its fair play and anti-discrimination activities are geared towards an equal society which uses the game to bridge all divides.

It is to the credit of FIFA that football is such a worldwide phenomenon in today's age. The World Cup's expansion of its horizons from having Europe and the Americas as its hosts to moving out to Asia and Africa in the twenty-first century has helped the sport gain increased global popularity.

Sepp Blatter, FIFA's eighth president, was largely responsible for spreading the World Cup's wings to reach new frontiers of Asia (in 2002)[30] and Africa (in 2010) that took the game away from confines of the Europeans and Americas. Blatter's reign, and the one of Joao Havelange that preceded it, was however mired with accusations of financial irregularity and labels of an unethical federation. However, to their credit, football did grow by leaps and bounds during the tenures of both Havelange and Blatter. Back home in India, FIFA was extremely supportive of the Indian federation in its effort to establish the sport back firmly in the country. The support from FIFA was recognised by AIFF as critical and AIFF's general secretary, Kushal Das, said in May 2015,[31] 'What's being reported about FIFA and Blatter from Europe is not

---

[29] fifa.com/fifa-world-ranking/ranking-table/men/
[30] https://www.theguardian.com/commentisfree/2015/may/31/fifa-sepp-blatter-champion-world-football-africa-asia
[31] https://www.theguardian.com/commentisfree/2015/may/31/fifa-sepp-blatter-champion-world-football-africa-asia

something that we in Indian football recognise. FIFA has been extremely supportive of us; without them we would be nowhere. It is a fantastic organisation and they are doing a wonderful job to grow the game in India and around the world,' suggesting that FIFA's story went beyond the grievances of the powerful European football nations.

Countries like India that have previously suffered or are currently suffering from funding problems to improve the state of the game are well-supported by FIFA via its financial outlays to developing nations. India, for example, received eight million pounds from FIFA in the three years leading up to 2015, funds that were used to improve infrastructure, and in various grassroots development activities. Artificial pitches in various Indian states like Meghalaya, Manipur, Goa, Maharashtra were built as part of the FIFA programme. It is because of FIFA's constant support that India has now emerged as a football destination, as the Under-17 World Cup exhibit in 2017. One thing is certain that without its aid, football would have still been confined to the elite European and American members, with those from other confederations largely consigned to the periphery.

★

Football has long been used as a socio-political bargaining chip due to its ability to drive the masses. The social significance of football was also seen in India during the British Raj when any and every victory by an Indian club over its British counterpart resulted in widespread euphoria. The connotations can be explained with the help of Mohun Bagan's win over East Yorkshire Regiment in the 1911 IFA Shield. Such was the importance of that victory that it changed an entire country's perception towards its rulers. Whereas, in the late nineteenth century, the Parsees learned and accepted the British norms of playing cricket, Bagan's win cemented the notion in the Indian psyche that playing barefoot is the way forward when it clearly was not.

A few years after Bagan's triumph in 1911, adidas founder, Adolf Dassler, gave birth to a sports shoes company in 1926 that has now become a behemoth. While Dassler was making footwear for the legendary Jesse Owens at the 1936 Berlin Olympics where he would win four gold medals, Indian football was having a glorious time with the rise of Mohammedan SC. Mohammedan—the Muslim-only Calcutta club—which would dominate Indian football in the 1930s, effectively suggested the end was near for the ruling Brits. And it did so playing barefoot, further enhancing the myth that boots are not a guarantee of success. West Germany won the World Cup in Germany wearing adidas boots, while according to some sources and legends, India's strong belief about playing barefoot led to it missing out on two World Cup appearances. This claim hasn't really been substantiated, and causes of India missing the World Cup were perhaps something else. It can only be speculated that India would definitely have played plenty of World Cups had it taken the other route.

In the meantime, other parts of the football world embraced the sport with greater enthusiasm. While the British introduced football to India post the 1850s, Brazil was introduced to the sport much later. In the ensuing years, Brazil has played in every World Cup, winning on five occasions, while India has never made a World Cup appearance. Brazil, however, was not the first South American country the British took football into. Uruguay and Argentina were early adopters of the sport too. The prominence of Uruguay in football's early days can be gauged by its dominance in the 1920s when it won two Olympic football tournaments, and the inaugural World Cup in 1930. The Spanish dictator, General Francisco Franco's military rule in the aftermath of the Second World War shaped the fate of Spanish football in the form of the El Clasico rivalry that we know. Match fixing in the German Bundesliga, mere eight years after the league's inception in 1963, where players and club presidents circumvented the rules of player licensing to throw matches and remain in the professional top flight, was a big dent to the introduction of professionalism. Those controversial events of the past have had a big say in our perspective towards contemporary football.

The more recent *Calciopoli* scandal in Italy exposed the dirty underbelly of elite European football, where even referees were deemed to have been bought. Despite the odds, Italy won the World Cup the same year Italian clubs Juventus, AC Milan, Fiorentina, Lazio and Reggina were convicted in the match fixing scandal in 2006, showing how the spirit of a collective in Football can overwhelm even the biggest of threats. In Italy's 2006 World Cup-winning squad, five players were from Juventus, including the captain Fabio Cannavaro. Despite FIFA's continued efforts, there is always the scope for malpractice given the sums of money involved.

Racism, a worldwide societal and political problem, continues to raise its ugly head in the sport of football. With the mass support and following that football enjoys, racism continues to exist in certain parts of the world. Raising its ugly head now and then, racism, along with fan violence is the biggest factor authorities continue to fight. Fan violence, like in the 1985 European Cup final at the Heysel Stadium in Belgium, continues to blight world football. Over the past few years, awarding of FIFA World Cup rights has also become a huge controversy along with various other charges of malpractice that have been levied on sports governing bodies across the world.

★

The English Premier League is the top division football league in England. It replaced the erstwhile English First Division in 1992 and changed the face of football. Football became more than a battle of twenty-two players on a pitch for ninety minutes with the advent of the Premier League. With the boom that came after the Premier League, football started capturing newer markets, India being among them. The English Premiership, as the Premier League was called back then, was first televised live in India on the

ESPN network in the 2001–02 season.[32] Today, every top league from across the world is telecast live on Indian television. Not only the Premier League, but also the Champions League and La Liga enjoy massive following in India, so much so that special events are organised in the country before big games like a final or a derby to promote them as well as create brand awareness. The UEFA Champions League final is undoubtedly the biggest draw, with La Liga's El Clasico not too far behind.

The Premier League entertains a very large fan base round the year in India and across the world, as do the other top leagues where the world's best players play. No Indian footballer has ever played on those elite stages, but the gap is slowly but surely being bridged, gradually boosting India's chances of a global appearance or its players' moves to the biggest clubs. Earlier, world stage football came to India every four years. The World Cup was the biggest attraction, mainly because it was broadcast in the free-to-air Doordarshan network. Hence, it is no surprise that the older generations in West Bengal—arguably India's football capital—are still hardcore fans of Brazil and Argentina. At the time television set its foot in India in the early 1980s, Brazil had been three times World Cup champions, riding on the back of Pele's majestic displays, and Argentina had won the 1978 World Cup and would go on to win the 1986 edition as well. Brazil and Argentina's success on the world stage left a psychological imprint in audio-visual format on the watching Indians. In fact, the 1986 World Cup in Mexico was the first World Cup that was telecast in its entirety on Indian television. According to the eminent Indian football writer Sharda Ugra,[33] World Cup football first entered Indian television

---

[32] http://timesofindia.indiatimes.com/ESPN-to-telecast-Premier-League/articles how/1964583945.cms

[33] https://qz.com/221760/india-could-have-a-decent-team-together-by-world-cup-2018/

sets during the knockout rounds of the 1982 World Cup. Even today, people jump for joy at the mention of Maradona.

A Liverpool vs West Ham United kick-off in the afternoon of 21 August 2001 kick-started the Premier League revolution in India. ESPN-Star Sports beamed the match live to Indian audiences and thus started something that has grown exponentially in the past sixteen years. With the internet boom that swept the world in the late 1990s and the early 2000s, there was a significant shot in the arm with the inception of social media. Nowadays, organisations, football clubs included, share important information first on social media. From free-to-air broadcasts to live streaming on one's mobile, personal computers or pubs screening live games, consuming football has never been so easy.

2018–19 is a landmark season for Spain's top division La Liga with social media giants Facebook taking its broadcast rights for India which it now shows on the Facebook platform for free.[34] Facebook then offered selective matches to Sony ESPN to be shown on television. Facebook had earlier attempted unsuccessfully to bid for Cricket's Indian Premier League broadcast rights.

Elite football clubs are starting to invest in fan engagement all across the world with specific focus towards India. Clubs from across the world and especially Europe are now looking to capture the imagination and staunch support of the fans in India with content specifically generated for Indian audiences along with posts in regional languages.

★

With the success of the Premier League in India, and the subsequent entry of other European competitions and leagues like the Champions League and La Liga into the Indian psyche, European

---

[34] https://www.theguardian.com/technology/2018/aug/14/facebook-buys-rights-la-liga-spanish-football-games-india-barcelona-lionel-messi

clubs are now targeting specific demographics of the Indian population to increase their following in the country. Residential programmes of various elite clubs are now regularly sprouting up across India as Indian football has joined hands with Western football. English giants, Liverpool and Arsenal, European heavyweights, Barcelona and Paris Saint-Germain, and Argentina outfit Boca Juniors have set up football schools in India. Apart from that, clubs are constantly coming up with customised content for their Indian audience.

La Liga World was brought to India with La Liga Girona FC taking on Indian Super League Kerala Blasters and Australian A League Melbourne City in a three game tournament in Kochi in July–August 2018. Two German clubs have visited India with playing squads in the last few years, and in future India will surely see a steady influx of big foreign teams play pre-season friendlies in the country. To that end, the improvement in infrastructure forced by the Indian Super League and FIFA Under-17 World Cup promises to see India have state-of-the-art facilities that will attract the biggest businesses of world football to explore the country and the opportunities that it brings in greater depth in the coming years.

Various Indian Super League franchises also have had tie-ups with big international clubs in the past though those partnerships so far haven't seen any long-term benefit. Two-time ISL champion Atletico de Kolkata derived their colours and stripes from its founding partner club Atletico Madrid.[35] Atletico Madrid incidentally now partner ISL new entrant Jamshedpur FC through a partnership formed in 2018. FC Pune City, another ISL franchise, entered into a partnership with Italian club Fiorentina and inherited, in part, the violet colour of its parent club along with orange which represents the state of Maharashtra where the FC Pune City is based. Delhi Dynamos is another ISL club which

---

[35] http://en.atleticodemadrid.com/noticias/atletico-de-madrid-to-establish-a-franchise-in-india

has had tie-ups with European clubs. Current Dutch champion Feyenoord[36] was its partner club in 2014, while the Premier League's West Bromwich Albion[37] also had a one season long technical agreement[38] with Delhi Dynamos in 2015. Furthermore, in April 2017, Spanish club Valencia also explored[39] opportunities to invest in the grassroots level of Indian football with the help of the Chennai Football Association. Apart from that, the AIFF has also collaborated with the German,[40] French,[41] Australian,[42] Dutch and Japanese[43] football associations as well as the Brazilian club, Atletico Paranaense.[44] All these are strategic tie-ups that aim to help develop Indian football with a bottom-up approach, focussing primarily on strengthening the base of the sport.

Such associations of fabled and historically rich foreign clubs as well as national teams with India and its clubs suggest that Indian football is no longer in the shadows. India has become a major player in global football circles and the continued foreign involvement promises to break the present status quo of the game in the ensuing years.

---

[36] http://timesofindia.indiatimes.com/sports/football/indian-super-league/top-stories/Guwahati-franchise-ropes-in-Spanish-World-Cup-winner-Capdevila/articleshow/38485445.cms
[37] https://www.wba.co.uk/news/2016/september/albion-1-delhi-dynamos-0/
[38] http://www.skysports.com/football/news/11698/10243792/west-brom-launch-initiative-with-indian-super-league-side-delhi-dynamos
[39] http://timesofindia.indiatimes.com/city/chennai/spanish-football-club-valencia-plans-academy-in-chennai/articleshow/58038886.cms
[40] https://www.the-aiff.com/news-center-details.htm?id=6408
[41] https://www.the-aiff.com/news-center-details.htm?id=6537
[42] https://www.the-aiff.com/news-center-details.htm?id=5317
[43] https://www.the-aiff.com/news-center-details.htm?id=6229
[44] https://www.the-aiff.com/news-center-details.htm?id=6054

CHAPTER 2
HISTORY OF FOOTBALL IN INDIA

Football in India was brought by the British, who ruled the country from 1858 to 1947 under the British Crown (large parts of the country were under the East India Company before that).[1] It was the British who introduced football to a majority of the non-European countries that play the sport today.

During the early days of the British Raj, the sport of football was exclusive only to the people of British origin, but so exciting was the sport that the Indian population fell in love with it. Various regimental teams of the British cavalry took part in tournaments like the Durand Cup and that is how the IFA Shield was incepted. These tournaments are among the oldest surviving football cup competitions in the world today. However, the British could not prevent the pervasion of football in the locals of their capital city of Calcutta, leading to numerous football clubs springing up during the late 1880s.

As mentioned earlier, Mohun Bagan was founded in 1889, making it the oldest club in the top division of Indian football. Mohammedan Sporting, a strong Calcutta Football League Club, is currently playing in I-League 2. The club that drives the emotions of West Bengal's Muslim community enjoyed a glorious period of success in the 1930s and 1940s. It became the first native club to win the Calcutta Football League[2]—a local Calcutta league started by the IFA in 1898. It set numerous records in the period between 1934 and 1942. The club's hegemony over a sustained period of time clearly registers as a landmark in Indian football. It was as if Mohammedan was unstoppable till the rise of another Kolkata giant. East Bengal, a club formed in 1920 after officials of Jorabagan Sports Club defected over a contentious decision regarding the playing eleven for a match against Mohun Bagan to form a

---

[1] https://en.wikipedia.org/wiki/British_Raj
[2] http://www.thehardtackle.com/2011/legends-of-indian-football-mohammedan-sporting-in-1930s/

new club, had very little in terms of early success. But it began to assert itself as an eminent force in Indian football when it broke Mohammedan's domestic supremacy to wrest control of the power battle in Calcutta.

A large part of the reason for formation of these clubs was to present the youth with a strong sense of belonging to Bengal and India. It would not be way off to say that that played an important role in the country's freedom movement which eventually led to Indian Independence in 1947. The social and political significance of football in India has been captured by the history of the three big Kolkata clubs. Their advent and subsequent successes can be truly said to be the beginning of Indian football; they were the clubs that truly got football kicking in India, along with other clubs in Kolkata like Town Club, Kumartuli Institute and Aryan Club which were established earlier than Mohun Bagan, Mohammedan Sporting and East Bengal but did not really make the impact that this troika did. The rest of the country followed soon after. India would have been affiliated to FIFA in 1948, however, its success on the international stage was still some way off.

Many new clubs came into existence during the first half of the twentieth century in West Bengal, but the three-way rivalry between Bagan, Mohammedan and East Bengal was the essence of Calcutta football. That said, Indian football's early days were not just about West Bengal and Calcutta's big three. Goa, a small state on the western coastline of India, was quickly becoming the footballing hub of the country with its distinctive Portuguese cultural influence. The Portuguese state of India survived for as long as 456 years, giving the regions under it, Goa included, a new cultural identity, different from other parts of India. That manifests in the popularity of football in Goa, where the sport is a major industry apart from mining and tourism. Likewise, other parts of India also warmed to the sport over the subsequent years. Today, we consider Kerala, Goa, West Bengal, Punjab, North-East Indian states like Manipur, Mizoram, Meghalaya, Sikkim and Assam as

Indian football's nerve centres. In about 150 years after the British introduced football to India, the game has only grown in the country. The hosting of the FIFA Under-17 World Cup 2017 by India was another staging post in the country's quest to become a superpower.

★

India has a rich history of sport and its origin in the country dates back to the Vedic era. Sports like badminton, chess, playing cards, snakes and ladders originated in India, but the more popular sports like cricket and football were inherited from external influences. Football, as cited earlier, got kicking in India following the arrival of the British in the mid-nineteenth century. Football, as well as other team sports were considered important to maintain the physical fitness levels of various artillery and regimental units of the empire. Football historian, Jonathan Wilson, notes that brilliantly in his book, *Inverting the Pyramid*, 'Team sports, it was thought, were to be promoted, because they discouraged solipsism, and solipsism allowed masturbation to flourish, and there could be nothing more debilitating than that.' The reverend Edward Thring, headmaster of Uppingham School, for instance, insisted in a sermon that it would lead to 'early and dishonoured graves'. Football was seen as the perfect antidote, because as EAC Thompson would write in *The Boys' Champion Story* paper in 1901, 'There is no more manly sport than football. It is so peculiarly and typically British, demanding pluck, coolness and endurance.'

There are very good politico-economic reasons for the coincidence, but there is also a neat symbolism in the fact that, after football had been used to shore up the empire, Britain's ultimate decline as an imperial power coincided with the erosion of the football superiority of the home nations. The last sentence is an apt description of what unfolded in India as well; the political implications of Mohun Bagan's 1911 IFA Shield win can never be overlooked.

★

Bagan's win in the 1911 IFA Shield final signalled a shift in the political scenario of India. At a time when the freedom movement was deflating, the Mariners'(as Mohun Bagan was nicknamed) triumph reinvigorated an entire nation and made them believe. Therefore, the social significance of Indian football can never be ignored. Football started to grow in prominence in Kolkata after Bagan showed the way. Mohammedan Sporting was wildly successful in the 1930s and 1940s and East Bengal started dominating thereafter. Bagan also started to bag the big honours after their first CFL title win in 1939, thereby creating a three-way axis that would dominate Kolkata football till the present day. Previously Calcutta became the nerve centre of football in India because of it being the capital of the British Empire in India. However, that same control centre of the British Raj brought about the eventual end of the empire. India would only join FIFA after independence and it played its first official match at the 1948 Olympics, as a nation free from colonisation.

'For about a decade, 1951 to 1962, India were among the best in Asia, winning the Asian Games gold medal twice, in 1951 at Delhi and 1962 at Jakarta,' eminent Indian football pundit, Novy Kapadia, wrote in 2011[3] about the rollercoaster journey of India as an international football team. 'India were also runners up in the prestigious Merdeka Football Tournament in Kuala Lumpur twice in 1959 and 1964 and runners up in the Asia Cup in Israel in 1964. India finished fourth in the 1956 Melbourne Olympics.' We were the first Asian nation to reach the Olympic football semi-final. In 1956, India beat Australia 4-2 in the Quarter-Finals and centre forward Neville D'Souza became the first and till now the only Asian to score a hat trick in the Olympics. From 1948 to 1960 India played regularly and with reasonable distinction in every Olympics. India also won the Quadrangular Tournament (beating

---

[3] http://www.thesundayindian.com/en/story/what-ails-indian-football/167/18897/

other contestants, Burma, Pakistan and Ceylon) four times from 1952 to 1955.

However, in the last three decades successes have been limited. Since 1960, India has not qualified for the Olympics and never made it to the World Cup finals. The last Asian Games quarter-final appearance was in Delhi in 1982. A bronze medal in the 1970 Bangkok Asian Games and joint winners with Iran in the Asian Youth Championship in 1974 are the only achievements at the continental level. Lack of international success had led to a decline in media and spectator interest in Indian football. In the twentieth century, many Indian footballers were among the best in Asia. Jarnail Singh, Chuni Goswami, PK Banerjee, T Balaram, Peter Thangaraj, Altaf Ahmed and Yusuf Khan, to name a few, have played for the Asian All Stars. Right back Sudhir Karmakar was chosen the Best Defender in Asia after the 1970 Bangkok Asiad. Such charismatic players attracted large crowds. Bhaichung Bhutia, who played in England's professional league for the second division Bury FC, and IM Vijayan were the last crowd-pulling footballers.

In its fairly long post-independence history, India has had only a few trophies at the international level to boast about. The indifferent performances of India on the international stage could be attributed to the ad hoc way football was run in the country for many decades. By the time a fairly professional setup was established to run football in the country, Brazil had won five FIFA World Cups inspired mainly by a strong culture, great interest in the sport and good organisation and management. Football in India has grown by leaps and bounds since it was first introduced to the country, but the rate of growth has been painstakingly slow compared to the rest of the world. However, recent signs suggest that India will soon be knocking on the doors of the biggest influencers in the football world, and its national team hopefully will dine at the World Cup table in the near future.

'Soccer played an important role in India's independence movement, generating a sense of national pride. A match in 1911 in which an Indian soccer team beat an English club to win an all-India tournament is still celebrated as a moment of national awakening,' wrote[4] Patrick Reevell in *The New York Times* in 2014, signifying the importance of a famous victory that set the tone for a greater victory, thirty-six years later. Mohun Bagan, Asia's oldest football club,[5] first participated in the IFA Shield only in 1909. The Mariners' had won[6] a few less prestigious titles like the Cooch Behar Cup, Trades Cup and Lakshibilas Cup before their IFA Shield bow in 1909. However, what transpired two years later has since changed the dynamics of football in India as a tool with social, political and economic connotations. Indian football historian, Kaushik Bandhyopadhyay, explains the consequences of that 1911 IFA Shield final, 'That kind of destroyed the impression of invincibility of the British. Football became a way for Indians to show their worth, as manly, as against European imagery of Bengalis as womanly.' Not only did the win quash myths of British superiority, but it was also a tremendous psychological boost to a country that needed it to resurrect its freedom movement against colonialism.

Mohun Bagan did not win another IFA Shield until after India gained independence in 1947, but its one Shield win on the afternoon of 29 July 1911 was enough to inspire countless Indian youth to stand up to the might of the British, something that eventually contributed to a successful independence movement for the country. Well over 80,000 people packed the Calcutta Football Ground[7] to see their beloved Mohun Bagan take on East Yorkshire Regiment on a hot July afternoon. Bagan, who had

---

[4] https://www.nytimes.com/2014/11/28/sports/soccer/new-indian-soccer-league-tries-glamour-approach.html
[5] http://inbedwithmaradona.com/journal/2011/2/23/the-immortal-xi-indian-nationalism.html
[6] http://www.mohunbaganclub.com/trophy-room/
[7] https://thefield.scroll.in/812760/remember-this-date-in-1911-when-mohun-bagan-beat-a-british-football-team-to-become-national-icons

beaten St Xavier's College, Rangers Football Club, Rifle Brigade and the first Middlesex Regiment en route to the final, was the rank outsider in the contest. Until 1911, no football club of eleven Indian players had ever won the IFA Shield. The eleven[8] that took to the field in the final—Hiralal Mukherjee, Bhuti Sukul, Sudhir Kumar Chatterjee, Manmohon Mukherjee, Rajendranath Sengupta, Nilmadhab Bhattacharya, Jatindranath Roy (Kanu), Srischanda Sarkar (Habul), Abhilash Ghosh, Bijaydas Bhaduri, Shibdas Bhaduri—have been immortalised in the annals of Indian football, but it was all a result of an endless struggle against the odds for the team of Bengalis. As the final played out in front of thousands of passionate fans, the team of foreigners were winning with only two minutes of the regulation 90 minutes remaining. What came about in the final two minutes were two goals from Shibdas Bhaduri and Abhilash Ghosh that turned the match around at the death, invoking jubilant scenes that marked the first victory in India's quest for a country free of the ruling British.

The 1911 IFA Shield final received widespread coverage, with British publications carrying the incredible story of a team of barefooted upstarts upsetting the more fancied regiment team. 'A team of Bengalees won the Football Association Shield in India after defeating the crack teams of three British Regiments amidst the applause of 80,000 of their countrymen. There is no reason of course to be surprised. Victory of association football goes to the side with the greatest physical fitness, the quickest eye, and the keenest wit,' was the *Manchester Guardian*'s take on the final that changed the course of Indian history. So important was Mohun Bagan's win in the wider context of Indian football that even its fiercest rival, East Bengal, acknowledges the Mariners' contribution to the country on its official website.[9] 'In the early part of twentieth

---

[8] http://www.thehardtackle.com/2010/history-of-mohun-bagan-chapter-1-the-origin-and-the-success-that-changed-indian-football/
[9] http://eastbengalfootballclub.com/legacy.php

century, football had been a popular sport among the Bengali youth—even more after Mohun Bagan's historic success in the 1911 IFA Shield final.'

★

India is home to some of the oldest cup competitions in world football. The Durand Cup, started in 1888, is the oldest tournament in Indian football, while the IFA Shield, the Rovers Cup and the Calcutta Football League followed suit soon after. Tournament culture in Indian football was prominent in Kolkata in the beginning but it spread to other parts of the country as well with the passage of time. The Bombay League first began in 1902 as the Harwood League. The information[10] furnished in the Rec.Sport. Soccer Statistics Foundation database on the league says, 'The earliest editions were organised by Colonel JG Harwood (RAMC), who was also the founding president of the Western India Football Association (WIFA) founded in September 1902. However, this association dissolved and the Harwood league and Rovers tournament were organised by separate committees until 1911, when a second incarnation of the WIFA was formed to govern football in the region. Some modern sources suggest that the league was only named after Colonel Harwood in later years, but newspaper reports from the period indicate otherwise. The league was referred to in the majority of reports as "The Harwood League" even from its first edition in 1902. As with all competitions in colonial India, the league was dominated by British army regimental teams in its first few decades. The first native Indian team to win the league was the Western India Automobile Association Staff team in 1942. In later years, disputes developed between competing associations attempting to organise competitions in the Bombay region, and during the 1990s there were two competing leagues, only one of which retained the Harwood League name; the major clubs gravitated

---

[10] http://www.rsssf.com/nersssf.html

towards the other more prestigious league. The two rival leagues were reunited in 2000. Bombay was renamed Mumbai in 1996.'

The Bombay League was the second regional league in India after the Calcutta Football League. Both leagues were initially restricted only to the British; native clubs started winning regularly as the empire crumbled. In 1942, five years before India achieved independence, Western India Automobile Association Staff became the first Indian winner of the Bombay League. Likewise, in Calcutta, Indian clubs only started winning the CFL on a regular basis after Mohammedan Sporting's unprecedented success in the 1930s. Mohammedan won seven CFL titles in eight years that would start a big three hegemony on the elite league of West Bengal. Since 1981, the CFL has been won by Mohun Bagan and East Bengal only. Mohammedan was the winner in 1981. The Delhi League and Goa League followed Bombay and Calcutta in the years after India's independence in 1947. 1948 saw the advent of the Delhi League while Goa followed suit soon after. Seventeen clubs have won the Delhi League so far, with New Delhi Heroes being the most successful one. In Goa, Salgaocar Sports Club and Dempo are the two most successful clubs. Dempo is the most successful national champion as well. As we can see, clubs from outside the power corridors started to emerge on the national scene after India's independence, gradually leading to a proliferation of football in newer states and regions. Dempo's rise as a force in the years after its formation in 1967, led to the club win of five national titles added to wins in the Federation Cup and the Goan state league. In 2017, Dempo celebrated its fiftieth anniversary.

Regional and state leagues had been the primary football tournaments in Indian football until the inception of the National Football League in 1996. The league ran for ten years before it was rebranded as the I-League in 2006. The I-League is still the top division national football league of India, and Dempo Sports Club of Goa, who does not play in the I-League anymore, has won it the most number of times. Mohun Bagan has won the national league four times, a pointer of their continued dominance of the domestic Indian football scene. The national league, however, is a relatively newer competition compared to the oldest Indian cup competitions. The Federation Cup was the biggest cup competition in Indian football till the 2016–17 season with the country's top teams participating in the week-long annual tournament. The Federation Cup was established in 1977 by the AIFF. Mohun Bagan and East Bengal are the two most successful teams in Federation Cup history, another reminder of Kolkata's shadow over Indian football. The Santosh Trophy is another popular cup competition staged annually pitting regional state associations and government institutions against each other. Initiated in 1946, the Santosh Trophy was once the most prestigious tournament in Indian football before the advent of the Federation Cup and the National Football League.

Football in the early days was not a professional sport as it is now; same was the case with India. The National Football League started as a semi-professional league in 1996, fairly late by international standards. Multimillion dollars' worth of transfers were being conducted in Europe, while India was still to wake up from its slumber.

In 1997, FC Kochin became the first fully professional football club to be established in India. The club from Kerala was bankrolled by PV Paul, Thomas Kannukkaadan and an NRI friend, and lured star players from India and abroad by offering high wages. The club had early success in the form of a Durand Cup win in its first year of formation, beating heavyweight Mohun Bagan in the final. FC Kochin's arrival signalled a change in the professional football scene in India. However, the club's subsequent financial mismanagement and eventual folding in 2004 brought dark clouds over the professional game. MG Radhakrishnan wrote in 2002,[11] 'The club's rise and decline have been swift; in the first

---

[11] http://indiatoday.intoday.in/story/first-indian-professional-football-club-fc-kochin-faces-closure-as-players-migrate/1/219886.html

six months of its creation in 1997, it won the country's oldest football championship, the Durand Cup, by beating the country's oldest club, Mohun Bagan, and also reached the finals of three major tournaments. When the first NFL was formed, FCK finished fourth. Now, the club has hit rock-bottom. Its best players have moved to other clubs, eleven top players leaving during the league season itself.'

The I-League's inception in 2007 by retooling the National Football League finally established full professionalism. Looking through this lens, India's non-participation in a FIFA World Cup can be attributed to its slowness in embracing the best practices of professional football world over. Whether it be playing with boots or introducing professionalism, India has always been a step or two behind the successful football nations. Scotland, one among them, has a long football history but has struggled on the international scene just like India. The two countries have a history as well, in the form of a player.

★

As is the case with most Indian football pioneers, Mohammed Salim hailed from Calcutta, the erstwhile capital of the British Empire in India. Salim's exploits on the football pitch with Mohammedan's relentless title winners of the 1930s led to him being invited to England for two friendly matches. Mihir Bose, with the help of Indian football historian Boria Majumdar, told Salim's story in *The Telegraph* in 2003,[12] 'After the title win of 1936, Salim was invited to play two friendlies against the Chinese Olympic side. A cousin called Hasheem who lived in England, and was then visiting Calcutta, witnessed the first match. Having seen Salim's exceptional display, Hasheem urged Salim to try his hand at European football. Hasheem was so persuasive that instead

---

[12] http://www.telegraph.co.uk/sport/2404435/A-unique-import-thrilled-Celtic-fans-back-in-the-1930s.html

of playing in the second Chinese friendly, Salim sailed with him on the City of Cairo for England. After a few days in London, Hasheem took him to Glasgow and Celtic Park. Salim was surprised to note that all the Celtic players were professionals. However, when asked whether he would be able to compete with them he nodded. Salim's confidence encouraged Hasheem to speak to Willie Maley, the Celtic manager. Hasheem told him, "A great player from India has come by ship. Will you please take his trial? But there is a slight problem. Salim plays in bare feet." Maley laughed as the idea of a barefooted amateur from India competing against Scottish professionals was difficult to believe. But Hasheem was persistent and the Celtic manager agreed to give him a trial. Salim was asked to demonstrate his skill before 1,000 club members and three registered coaches. Salim's ability, even in bare feet, astonished them. They decided to play him in a match against Hamilton. Salim, barefooted, proved exceptional helping Celtic win 5-1.'

In his second match against Galston, Celtic won 7-1 and his performance led *The Scottish Daily Express* of 29 August 1936, to carry the headline, 'Indian Juggler—New Style.' The paper wrote, 'Ten twinkling toes of Salim, Celtic FC's player from India, hypnotised the crowd at Parkhead last night. He balances the ball on his big toe, lets it run down the scale to his little toe, twirls it, hops on one foot around the defender.'

However, after a few months in Scotland, Salim began to feel homesick and was determined to return to India. The exact cause of his return has not really been verified but is largely attributed to his inability to adapt to a new country and culture which did not make him feel at home. Not many Indian footballers have gone on to play for foreign clubs since. A handful of them—Bhaichung Bhutia, Subrata Pal, Sunil Chhetri and Gurpreet Singh Sandhu—have played in foreign leagues until now. Gurpreet was the latest Indian to ply his trade with Norweigian side Stabaek and, in fact, even started their UEFA Europa League qualifier against

Welsh side Connah's Quay. He has since moved back to Bengaluru FC to play in the Indian Super League. More and more young Indian footballers are now going abroad for better exposure to high quality facilities, but the hero to fly the Indian flag in leagues abroad remains elusive for now. While Salim's achievement inspired countless generations in pre-independence India, the likes of Bhutia, IM Vijayan and Chhetri have been the heroes for the contemporary generation.

Talking about Indians playing abroad, female footballers have had more recent success than their male counterparts. Indian women footballers Tanvie Hans[13] and Aditi Chauhan have played in the UK lower divisions in the recent past, highlighting the fact that football is spread across India, irrespective of gender. Tanvie, who holds a British passport, and hence has been ineligible to play for the India National Team, played for both Tottenham and Fulham, while Indian National Team Keeper Aditi played for West Ham during her education stint in London.

★

We have discussed the impact of the Kolkata giants like East Bengal and Mohun Bagan, but other clubs were also as impactful in the sport of football growing in India. However, their impact came much later. While the Calcutta Football League was incepted by the IFA in 1898, local leagues in the country's other football pockets started more than half a century later. The present-day football hotbeds of India—Kerala, North-East India, Goa, Punjab—saw full-fledged leagues only after the 1950s. Goa, like West Bengal, was an early adopter of football owing to foreign influences.

The first league in the state of Goa was organised in 1951 by the Conselho de Desportos. The Goa Football Association (GFA) came into being a few years later in 1958 and football began to

---

[13] https://www.saddahaq.com/tanvie-hans-the-greatest-female-football-player-india-may-never-have

spread to every nook and corner of the state. The Goan league structure was patchy at best in its early years; it ran as the Goa First Division until 1977 when the GFA introduced the Goa Super League to supplant the First Division. The Super Division later rebranded to the Goa Professional League, which is a pioneer of professionalising football in India. As the great football clubs of West Bengal played an important role in identifying the game as a propaganda tool against British colonialism and laid the sport's early foundations in India, the state of Goa, inspired by its past Portuguese influence, took Indian football a notch higher. It followed in the footsteps of the prominent football nations and was the harbinger of professionalism in Indian football. Goa's profound impact on Indian football can be gauged by the fact that even today, no other Indian state has afforded full professional status to football apart from Goa.

Meanwhile, the Mumbai District Football Association (MDFA) had been running the MDFA Elite Division since the early 1900s, suggesting that the penetration of football in India was not confined to just a few states. Football was spreading all over India. From Karnataka and Kerala in the southern part of India to Punjab in northern India and the belt of eight north-eastern states, state leagues developed at an unprecedented rate. Although football is yet to reach every corner of India, it has now reached a level in the country where Indian football is a major stakeholder in the global game.

★

With India's reputation in world football as an underexplored region, elite teams from Europe and the Americas have, over the years, seen the country as an opportunity in waiting but never have they sustained their early impetus. Various international teams have visited India over the years, notch by notch raising the profile of the Indian game. While India started hosting international teams after their entry into FIFA in 1948, no European or American team had ever visited the country until 1977. It was in 1977 that a beleaguered Mohun Bagan side,[14] fresh from a 5-0 defeat to local rival East Bengal in the 1975 IFA Shield, conjured up a plan to host the triple World Cup winner and best footballer ever, Pele, with his North American Soccer League (NASL) team, New York Cosmos.

Some astute persuasion from the Indians saw Pele & Company come down to India. The Brazilian had retired from international football and was well past his peak but was the star attraction as Cosmos played a 2-2 draw with Mohun Bagan. That was the last time India would host an elite team or a top-class player like Pele until the new millennium. Neither would Indian footballers go abroad. In 2006, the AIFF agreed on a Memorandum of Understanding with the German Football League (DFL)[15] which led to the visit of Bayern Munich to India in 2008 as part of an Asian trip dubbed as 'Oliver Kahn's Farewell Tour'. The Mohun Bagan team comprising the likes of Sangram Mukherjee and Rakesh Masih faced a Bayern Munich side featuring the likes of legendary German goalkeeper Kahn, Toni Kroos and Mark van Bommel, going down 3-0 in a lopsided match. Four years later, in 2012,[16] Bayern Munich would visit India again for a match branded as the 'Audi Football Summit' to take on the Indian national team, for whom captain Bhaichung Bhutia would play his final career match. Bhutia endured a farewell to forget as Bayern ran through the Indians to win 4-0, every goal coming inside the first half.

While the visits of Cosmos and Bayern brought to India a plethora of stars like Pele, Kahn, Arjen Robben, Bastian Schweinsteiger, the subsequent years since 2012 have seen more

---

[14] http://timesofindia.indiatimes.com/sports/football/top-stories/How-Mohun-Bagan-pulled-off-the-Pele-coup-in-1977/articleshow/49318260.cms

[15] http://www.dw.com/en/made-in-germany-indias-steady-soccer-revolution/a-3823163

[16] http://timesofindia.indiatimes.com/sports/football/top-stories/Bayern-Munich-crush-India-4-0-in-Baichung-Bhutias-farewell-match/articleshow/11438618.cms

German clubs set up their base in India. TSG Hoffenheim, a Bundesliga club, made a trip to the north-east Indian state of Mizoram in 2014 with stars like Roberto Firmino and Eugen Polanski to play a Mizoram XI.[17] Yet again, the Indian side ended up losing, firing blanks in a 3-0 defeat. In between those matches, the Argentina national team featuring the genius Lionel Messi also toured India for a friendly against Venezuela in August 2011.[18] While the likes of Messi and Angel Di Maria were big draws, the match in general was drab as Argentina emerged 1-0 winner. In recent times, there have been discussions about India's growing potential as a football friendly destination but nothing has materialised until now. Since Hoffenheim's visit in 2014, football in the country has grown in different ways with the advent of the Indian Super League in 2014. 2018 saw Spanish La Liga team Girona FC and Australian team Melbourne City play the La Liga World Trohpy against Kerala Blasters in the football-mad state of Kerala.

The rise of Indian football has been palpable, with the legendary Arsenal manager Arsene Wenger prophesising India's ascent into a future superpower in January 2017,[19] 'I expect India to come to the [elite] game and I hope it will happen.' These are evident signs that Indian football is only moving forward.

We have seen how India is not among the front runners in world football, but the country is among the leaders in producing hand-stitched footballs. North Indian cities like Jalandhar and Meerut are the largest producers and suppliers of football equipment in India. A 2010 report in *The Wall Street Journal* read,[20] 'India is

---

[17] http://media.cpdfootball.de/2014/05/13/tsg-1899-hoffenheim-defeats-strong-mizoram-xi/
[18] http://www.goal.com/en-india/info/572/internationals/2011/08/31/1743699/lionel-messi-in-india-argentina-vs-venezuela-at-salt-lake
[19] http://www.independent.co.uk/sport/football/premier-league/arsenal-news-arsene-wenger-china-super-league-india-japan-burnley-a7535616.html
[20] https://blogs.wsj.com/indiarealtime/2010/04/28/new-sore-point-for-pakistan-india-soccer-balls/

competing with Pakistan directly on its home turf: the production of high-quality hand-stitched soccer balls. The Indian industry is actually an offshoot of the Pakistani one, which began in colonial times. After Partition, traditional soccer ball makers who left for India set up in Jalandhar, and then later in Meerut,' suggesting how the Indian equipment manufacturing industry has boomed amid the burst of Indian football on the global stage.

★

The Indian National Team is, as of August 2018, the ninety-sixth best football team according to FIFA's rankings, but rankings rarely matter at the top end of the competition. Every four years at the FIFA World Cup, the likes of Brazil, Germany and Italy will always be considered favourites because of their winning pedigree irrespective of FIFA rankings. India's highest ever FIFA ranking was ninety-fourth in 1996. It has only sporadically entered the FIFA top 100 since the inception of the rankings in August 1993. The Indian National Team's history is not littered with stories of glorious achievements, but it has won quite a few trophies nonetheless.

The Blue Tigers haven't won a whole host of trophies with six SAFF Championship titles their biggest haul. Starting with Balaidas Chatterjee's appointment in 1948, the national team has had eighteen different head coaches. Among them, Syed Nayeemuddin, Sukhwinder Singh and current Head Coach Stephen Constantine have taken charge of India on more than one occasion. Talking about success, India was among the foremost Asian nations in football in the years after independence. That period is still considered India's golden period in international football. After winning the Asian Games gold medal in 1951, India reached the semi-finals of the 1956 Melbourne Olympics and finished runner-up in the 1964 AFC Asian Cup, which rank as the greatest achievements in the national team's history. India also finished fourth at the 1958 Asiad in Tokyo during an era that is the most fruitful the national team has ever had.

HISTORY OF FOOTBALL IN INDIA 47

Indian Contingent during the opening ceremony of
1956 Melbourne Olympics

CHAPTER 3
REGIONAL GROWTH OF FOOTBALL

India is a unique country—a phenomenon difficult to witness anywhere else in the world. With every 200 km travelled in India in any direction, we see a change in the language (or at least the dialect), the food, the climate, people's appearance, even behaviour for that matter. Yet the country exists as one uniquely diversified yet unified country. With all its differences it still has the same fabric.

The growth of football in India then has to take a very regional flavour and how the beautiful game moved within India is a great story in itself. And the story of the ball moving around in India has to begin with Bengal—the undisputed capital of football in India.

BENGAL

It can be aptly said that the nerve centre for football in India is none other than the state of Bengal. Steeped in a rich history—179 years old—the erstwhile British state of Bengal and its capital Calcutta was where football took its first steps in the subcontinent. 'Natives' as the local 'Bengalee' people were known under the British, hardly got a sniff as football was considered to be an elite game, only to be enjoyed by the ruling class. It was in 1838, that Kolkata witnessed its first ever match recorded in history. Etonians triumphed over rest of Calcutta team 3-0. It was sixteen years later, that a game played between Calcutta Club of Civilians and Gentlemen of Barrackpore on 13 April 1854[1] is widely considered to be the match that defined Indian football for decades to come.

Nagendra Prasad Sarbadhikari and his friends first started playing the sport at the Hare School playground in 1877. He then went on to establish the first Indian football club, the Wellington Club in 1884—thus making him the 'Father of Indian Football'.

---

[1] Ronojoy Sen, *Nation at Play: A History of Sport in India* (Columbia University Press, 2013), p. 50.

Sadly, it went defunct within a year and the Shobhabazar Club sprang up in 1885,[2] patronised by Kumar Jishnendra Krishna Deb. Soon after, National Association and Town Club were also established in the very same year and suddenly Calcutta had its own bunch of Indian football clubs. While most folded soon after, Nagendra Prasad Sarbadhikari resurfaced to take charge of Shobhabazar Club, the only 'Native' club allowed to participate in the Trades Cup, the oldest football tournament of India.

The Trades Club introduced the tournament in 1879, a year after the club's inception, which was later rechristened to Dalhousie Athletic Club. In the 1892 edition, Shobhabazar Club faced East Surrey in the opening match, and for the first time in history, a 'Native' team had beaten a British side. Going forward, a newfound fervour was developed amongst the 'Bengalees' who took inspiration in their fight for freedom through the game of football.

Sir Umeshchandra Majumder (Sir Dukhiram) turned out to be the first guru of Indian football. He initiated the Students Union Club in 1887 at his residence—the Mohun Bagan Villa. A dispute amongst his peers later led to the disbanding of the club and two new clubs—Aryans and Mohun Bagan were formed in 1889 as a result. Players like Shibdas and Bijoydas Bhaduri, Balaidas Chatterjee, Surya Chakraborty, Kali Ghosh, Samad and few others started their football careers under the tutelage of Sir Dukhiram at Aryans. Thus, the trinity of Nagendra Prasad Sarbadhikari, Jishnendra Krishna Deb and Sir Dukhiram Majumder are considered to be the pioneers of Bengal football.

Parallelly, the Trades Cup grew immensely popular and the officials of Dalhousie Athletic Club and Calcutta Club came together to set up an association, envisaging an expanded version of the tournament in the future. The representatives of the British Clubs formed the Indian Football Association (IFA) in 1893. It was not until the turn of the century in 1900 that an Indian club had a

---

[2] Nirmal Nath, *History of Indian Football* (Readers Service, 2011), pp. 31–34.

trophy under its belt. The National Association of South Calcutta, under the guidance of Manmatha Ganguly won the Trades Cup, beating the British outfit, Shibpur Civil Engineering College in the final. *The Indian Daily News* reported on 11 August 1900, 'The match came off on the Shobhabazar ground last evening and attracted very large crowds.'[3] It was Manmatha Ganguly himself, who introduced the concept of playing with boots in 1902 to the local 'Bengalees' of the city.

The IFA had already sowed the seeds of Indian football in 1893 when it started the IFA Shield. Divided into two zones, the Western zone was played in Allahabad with four army teams and the Eastern zone was held at Calcutta with Dalhousie, Calcutta Club, Howrah United, Naval Volunteers (later known as Rangers Club), four army teams and Shobhabazar, the only 'Native' team. Another stepping stone was the induction of former Shobhabazar player Kalicharan Mitra in 1900 as the first Indian representative in the British dominated IFA. Manmatha Ganguly, in 1903, was offered the post of Joint Secretary, hence a sense of heterogeneity was achieved.

Between 1906 and 1908, Mohun Bagan registered a hat-trick of Trades Cup titles. Their performance was awarded with a place in the 1909 IFA Shield. In their IFA Shield debut, Bagan beat YMCA 4-0 but lost their subsequent games. Yet again, Bagan's campaign in the 1910 IFA Shield followed a similar pattern. After beating St. Xavier's 2-1 in the opening game, two defeats saw an early ouster from the tournament. Mohun Bagan were third time lucky and the final match went down in history of Indian footballing folklore worshipping the immortal eleven.[4]

In the season opener against St Xavier's,[5] yet again, Mohun Bagan could only field ten players and the handicapped team won

---

[3] (my emphasis)
[4] (my emphasis)
[5] Nirmal Nath, *History of Indian Football* (Readers Service, 2011), pp. 12–18.

by a convincing 3-0 margin. A rain soaked 2-0 win against Rangers Club followed, securing progression to the quarterfinals for the first time. Rifle Brigade, a team of army men stood in Mohun Bagan's way and a solitary goal by Bijoydas Bhaduri, ten minutes from time ensured Bagan had made it to the semi-finals.

1st Middlesex Regiment awaited them in the last four. The going was tough to start with as the opposition's goalkeeper Piggott had English top-flight football experience with Portsmouth before joining the army. Five minutes before the break, the British side broke the deadlock. A Kanu Roy goal enforced a replay, two days later on 26 July after his second half goal drew level. The gods smiled upon the brave Mohun Bagan team in the replay and owing to Piggott's injury, the Indian side scored three in the last ten minutes to set up a date with East Yorkshire Regiment from Faizabad. The date was 29 July 1911. The warm Saturday afternoon subsided to pave the way for an evening clear of the growing political tensions in Calcutta. Where there was widespread dissent against the British rule and extremist movements were quick to gather pace, the focus shifted to a game of football, where a British side were up against India's very own 'Natives' in the final of the IFA Shield.

The match fuelled a sense of nationalism as around 100,000 people had flocked to the Calcutta Football Club ground, travelling from neighbouring states of Bihar, Assam and the eastern part of Bengal. 'Till the semi-final, Mohun Bagan was only playing a football tournament. But as it geared up to meet East Yorkshire Regiment in the final, it seemed that the aspirations of the entire nation rested on its shoulders,' wrote eminent sports journalist Jaydeep Basu in his book *Stories from Indian Football*.[6]

The ground choc-a-bloc, for the spectators the only way to understand the proceedings in the ground was to look up at the sky where flying kites signalled the scoreline. A fifty-minute

---

[6] Jaydeep Basu, *Stories from Indian Football* (UBS Publishers' Distributors 2003), pp. 1–16.

game, and a black kite fluttered over the Calcutta skyline to announce Mohun Bagan were trailing at the end of the twenty-five minute first half. The hopes of a nation in struggle were buoyed in the second half as a green and maroon kite flew aloft five minutes from time. Shibdas Bhaduri found the elusive equaliser with a solo effort. With seconds to go in the clock, Shibdas again dribbled past defenders Jackson and Martin and was one-on-one with the goalkeeper Cressey. A pass to an unmarked Abhilash Ghosh and a simple right-footed push into the net gave birth to a fresh age in Indian football and consequently the struggle for freedom in India. The world took note that a team comprising of ten barefooted 'Bengalees' (Sudhir Chatterjee was the only one to wear boots) had outwitted a British outfit.

Reuters exclaimed, 'For the first time in the history of Indian football, an Indian team, the Mohun Bagan, consisting purely of "Bengalees", has won the IFA Shield, beating crack teams of English regiments… When it was known that the East Yorkshire Regiment had been beaten, the "Bengalees" were tearing off their shirts and waving them.'

London's *Daily Mail* wrote, 'It was a notable victory, gained over the best British regimental teams, and not even the sweltering heat of Calcutta to which the "Bengalees" are better insured than the white man, can discount it.' A nationalist local daily *Amrita Bazar Patrika*, came up with the defining headline, 'May God bless the Immortal Eleven of Mohun Bagan for raising their nation in the estimation of the Western people by their brilliant feat.'

The 'Bengalees' then witnessed a great Indian revolution in itself as people from all walks of life came together as one to bask in the triumph of Mohun Bagan. The priest of a Hindu temple showered blessings upon the players as Muslim youths joined the procession—there was no segregation by religion. Calcutta stood as a united Indian city on 29 July 1911. Such were the long-term ramifications in the political stratosphere which was coincidentally buoyed by the win that King George V, the emperor of India, had to shift the capital to Delhi from Calcutta, five months later on 12 December 1911.

Hiralal Mukherjee, Bhuti Sukul, Sudhir Chatterjee, Rajendranath Sengupta, Manmohan Mukherjee, Nilmadhab Bhattacharya, Sirishchandra 'Habul' Sarkar, Bijoydas Bhaduri, Jatindranath 'Kanu' Roy, Abhilash Ghosh and skipper Shibdas Bhaduri were names that were etched on the pages of Indian football history forever.

HYDERABAD

The Princely state of Hyderabad first hoisted the flag of football in southern India in the 1920s. The beautiful game had no shortage of patronage by the royalty, especially the Nawab of Tarband and the Maharajas of Kakinada and Rajahmundry. In 1939, a consolidated body of the Hyderabad Football Association was formed and that became the cradle of many talents which emerged in the Indian national team post-independence in 1947.

Syed Abdul Rahim, regarded as one of the best coaches of the national team till date, was the best gift Hyderabad ever presented to Indian football. However, it was the talismanic team City Afghans—the police team of Hyderabad—which rung the bells, winning the 1943 AshGold Cup Final in Bengaluru, beating Royal Air Force, which included England cricketer and Arsenal winger Denis Compton. Later renamed Hyderabad City Police (HCP) after independence, the black and yellow clad team won the 1950 Durand Cup (the first after Indian independence), beating Mohun Bagan, which included greats like T Aao, Sailen Manna and Abdus Sattar.

Hyderabad's influence grew the strongest in 1965 in the DCM Trophy final, where HCP had to square off against their own 'B' team, Central Police Lines. HCP which was renamed as

Late SA Rahim
Disclaimer: This image is for representation purpose only.

Andhra Pradesh Police housed the talent of Syed Nayeemuddin,[7] who later went on to coach the Indian and then the Bangladeshi national sides. His teacher during his schooldays, coincidentally, was Syed Abdul Rahim, whose tenure at the helm of the national team came to be known as the 'golden age' of football in India. Rated to be as shrewd as any other European coach, Syed Abdul Rahim still records the highest achievement by any Indian national team coach. Taking over in 1951, India dominated the inaugural Asian Games in New Delhi, winning gold. But the 1952 Helsinki Olympics turned sour as SA Rahim had a lot to ponder upon after a 10-1 thrashing by Yugoslavia, leading to an interim sacking,

---

[7] PP Surender Kumar, *Hyderabadi's Contribution to Indian Football.*

after beating Pakistan in a Quadrangular Tournament in Dacca. He came back stronger with new tactics he experimented in the local Hyderabad leagues and achieved a fourth-place finish in the 1956 Olympics in Melbourne, beating hosts Australia 2-4 in the quarterfinal after Hungary withdrew from the first round.

SA Rahim as a coach also had a silver medal in the 1959 Merdeka Cup and ended his career with yet another Asian Games title in 1962 at Jakarta. He passed away in 1963 but he had already unearthed talents like Tulsidas Balaraman (East Bengal legend and 1962 Asian Games gold winner) and Peter Thangaraj (India's goalkeeper extraordinaire) from his native state. Mohammad Habib too was a product of Hyderabad's footballing ecosystem, going on to turn out for all of Kolkata's big three—Mohun Bagan, East Bengal and Mohammedan Sporting.

For the better part of fifty years, the culture of football in present day Telangana and Andhra Pradesh remained in despair. Only in 2015, a professional club from the region emerged. Fateh Hyderabad AFC founded by Yogesh Maurya now plays

The Indian Football team that won gold medal in
1962 Asian Games in Jakarta

in the second division I-League, looking to return Hyderabad its past glory.

TAMIL NADU

During the British rule, two clubs—Pachaiyappa's Football Club and Tilak-Moti United Club were mostly being marauded by the British regimental team week-in, week-out, but their devoted nationalism and continued efforts to put up a show against the rulers gave a boost to the footballing fraternity in Madras.

Till 1933, football on the Coromandel Coast was unheard of until a Madras XI held a formidable IFA XI of Calcutta. Later that year, a formal body—Madras Football Association was formed under the aegis of a school headmaster, AM Kaniappa Mudaliar.[8] The vice-chancellor of the Madras University, Dr Lakshmanaswamy Mudaliar too joined him and both these educationists took on the mantle to change the scenario of the sport. The game began to grow and within years, the Madras City Corporation Commissioner, JPL Shenoy[9] gave the green light for the construction of a 44,000 seater multipurpose stadium, which is now the JL Nehru Stadium, shared between ISL side Chennaiyin FC and I-League team Chennai City FC (who incidentally after their first season moved to Coimbatore). Centre forward M Thangaraj and right back K Balagopal were at the peak of their prowess in the 50s when Wimco Club won the Senior Division six times in a row, from 1950 to 1955. The former was awarded with a spot in the Manila 1954 Asian Games squad. The same year, Madras hosted the Santosh Trophy for the first time, receiving acclaim for being excellent organisers, rare words heard in Indian football even in the twentieth century. M Thangaraj struck up a lethal partnership with

---

[8] Nirmal Nath, *History of Indian Football* (Readers Service, 2011), pp. 78-84.
[9] http://www.thehindu.com/society/history-and-culture/This-might-have-been-in-French/article15858192.ece

Bengal's Sheoo Mewalall and gelled well with most of his India teammates, after securing a move to East Bengal. Other Tamil Nadu greats included J Kittu and Simon Sundaraj.

Renamed in 1969 as Tamil Nadu Football Association, it used to organise many an age-group and senior football tournaments but most of them have shut operations for lack of funds. The TFA Shield and Vittal Trophy—two national level tournaments were held simultaneously but only the latter exists, albeit resurrected at the turn of the century. Tamil Nadu's football saw a glimmer of hope when the state team ended runners-up at the 2011–12 Santosh Trophy.

Indian Bank made the effort to shine on the national stage, though it wasn't till Chennaiyin FC was formed in 2014 with the advent of Indian Super League that a team from Chennai was seen regularly featuring in a national league. Not in the original line-up of the eight teams to be formed, Chennai saw the ISL team move at the last moment as noted actor Abhishek Bachchan, Indian cricketer Mahendra Singh Dhoni partnered Vita and Jalaj Dani to take ownership of the team. And what a fateful takeover that was. Chennaiyin has now won two out of the four Indian Super League Championships to become the most successful club in the ISL along with ATK.

KERALA

Chennai City entered the I-League as a corporate team in 2016–17 and have managed to hold their own while being faced with operational challenges, which meant moving their home base from Chennai to Coimbatore in 2017–18 season.

The Malabar area first saw widespread enthusiasm for football (though not much of it was recorded pre-independence), after the unification[10] of Travancore, Cochin and Malabar—when

---

[10] Srinivasa Iyengar, *History of the Tamils*, pp. 192–195.

the state of Kerala was born in 1956. Colonel Godavaram Raja of Trivandrum founded the Kerala Football Association and the game among the masses took off on an exponential scale. Even before that, the Malabar District Football Association (MDFA) XI participated in the 1954 Rovers Cup where a surprise win over BN Railway followed a lead of two goals over eventual champions Hyderabad City Police. The SA Rahim coached side fought back to win 3-2 but the crowd at the Cooperage Stadium in Bombay took note of the boys from the South. Slowly and steadily, Keralites made their way into the national team. Forward J Anthony and full back TA Rehman were the pioneers—both Olympians.[11] The Malabar region saw maximum representation with SS Narayanan and M Devadas in the late 50s.

Odampilly Chandrasekharan Menon, C Mustafa and TM Verghese (non-Malabar) were products of the strong district leagues in Kozhikode, Kannoor and Mallapuram, who were flying the Indian football flag high in the south. Sadly, most of the players moved on to either Calcutta or Bombay for better pay, with some moving to Goa, which was seeing the fag end of its Portuguese colonialism. January to May being the football season in Kerala, almost each district had its own all-India invitational tournament. The Sait Nagjee Trophy in Kozhikode is still running strong. Thrissur's Chackola Cup was a spectacle, mainly due to the trophy of 145 sovereigns, the costliest in India in its time. The Kerala crowd not only took inspiration from their local heroes but teams, especially from Bombay and Goa, like Caltex, Tata, Mahindra, Vasco, Sesa, Dempo used to capture the imagination of the youth. Modern heroes, IM Vijayan, VP Sathyan, Jo Paul Ancheri et al. were the real finds of these leagues.

However, after the nationalisation of the leagues, clubs from Kerala have had a topsy-turvy time at the top. While the office teams had run out of steam, negligible sponsorship also meant a decline of participants and thus signalled a lengthy lull of Kerala

---

[11] Nirmal Nath, *History of Indian Football* (Readers Service, 2011), pp. 69–77.

football the previous decade. It was surprising that the stupendous success of Thrissur-born IM Vijayan[12] did not spur many youngsters to excel in the sport from the region. 'Kalo Harin' or 'Black Buck' as he was christened during his Mohun Bagan days in Kolkata, formed a lethal partnership with Bhaichung Bhutia for the national team. Vijayan still remains one of the fastest goalscorers in an international game, needing only twelve seconds against Bhutan in 1999. He retired with seventy-nine international caps to go with his forty senior goals for India.

Football mad Kerala saw a revival in club football with god of cricket Sachin Tendulkar led Kerala Blasters establishing base in Kochi. Kerala Blasters also saw change of hands as its original bidders made way for Hyderabad-based Nimmagadda Prasad and also brought in superstars Chiranjeevi, Nagarjuna, Mohanlal to the ownership band. The move sparked great interest with Kochi stadium becoming the spectacle of the Indian Super League filling in record number of fans season on season. Club football at I-League level saw the respected Gokulam group bring in Gokulam Kerala FC as a corporate entry from the 2017–18 season and FC Kerala play in the I-League 2 season along with Kerala Blasters Reserve team. The Blasters have made good use of their on-ground support, reaching finals of the Indian Super League twice, beaten by ATK both times in the finals. They remain the most supported club in Indian Super League and have a strong supporters group in Manjapada who have been consistently voted as the best supporter group.

BANGALORE (BENGALURU)

While many do not associate Bengaluru of old with football, contrarily, the game had its beginnings in the city when Indians took on Italian prisoners of war during World War II. In the 1920s and 30s football was popular both in the Bangalore Cantonment

---

[12] http://www.thehardtackle.com/2012/i-m-vijayan-indian-footballs-best-striker-tht-heros/

(Sullivan and Garrison grounds) and City areas (YMCA ground and Cubbonpet). Various members of the 1948 and 1952 Olympics India team were players who sharpened their skills on the Austin Town ground. T Shanmugham, Kannayan and Raman were the first ones. Soon KV Varadarajan, SA Basheer, MA Sattar, P Venkatesh, M Kempaiah and Ahmed Khan too emerged from the Cantonment area of the Garden City.

The British introduced two tournaments in the 1940s—The Stafford Cup and the AshGold Cup[13] which drew heavy crowds, mostly British expatriates during the Raj—helping the sport to grow into the city culture. Bangalore Muslims were the first non-Calcutta club to instil a sense of nationalism through the game from the erstwhile state of Mysore. In 1937, the team did a 29 July 1911 all over again as they won a blue ribbon tournament in Bombay as the first civilian team in the West to beat a British team by winning the Rovers Cup. They defended their title in a sweeter manner as they defeated British-based A&S Highlanders in the 1938 finals, as compared to Mohammedan Sporting the previous year. Local rivalry in the form of Bangalore Crescent developed in the mid-40s and the football scene in the city flourished. All this changed when the likes of Ahmed Khan and Abdus Sattar chose to move to Calcutta in quest of greener pastures. Other players joined industrial sides and the irreversible decline of Bangalore Muslims commenced in the 1950s. However, Mysore won the Santosh Trophy four times, each time beating Bengal in the finals in 1947, 1953, 1968 and 1969. Local teams were only made up by industries like ITI, HAL, BHEL, BEL, etc. which had considerable success but they were not inclined towards the sport primarily, focussing more on their business.

A few years ago, Brazilian legend Pele showed up in the form of a full-sized bronze statue in front of Bangalore Mars FC

---

[13] http://www.thehindu.com/thehindu/mp/2002/06/10/stories/2002061000270100.htm

in Gowthampura.[14] A true tribute to a place which has produced more than two hundred footballers including Arumainayagam and Shanmugham Venkatesh, the current assistant Coach of the Indian national men's senior team.

Bengaluru FC established in 2013, who were a direct entrant into the I-League and have since 2017 moved over to the ISL, have taken over the mantle of revolutionising not just Bengaluru football but also Indian football. Ozone group has come in with their football club, which competes in the second division of the I-League.

MUMBAI

In 1890, the Rovers Club was formed and the Rovers Cup started immediately, thus setting the pace for football in what is now the economic capital of India. The Bombay Football Association (BFA) saw the light of day in 1902, and the Harwood League began with seven teams, but was later discontinued.[15] In 1911, Rovers Club and BFA joined forces to be known as the Western India Football Association (WIFA). Just when the Harwood League was being revived again in 1914, World War I broke out and the Cooperage Stadium was in a lockdown, under the control of the Royal Army. After a lull of eight years, the Cooperage Stadium saw a ball being kicked again in 1921. The Rovers Cup became a beacon of a football tournament in the nation and the local Harwood League saw participation from all walks of life and religions from within the city. The first wave of success came under the leadership of Sanjeeva Utchil in 1954 when Bombay clinched the Santosh Trophy, beating Services 2-1 in the final in Madras after ending as runners-up earlier in 1945 and 1947. Names

---

[14] http://www.deccanchronicle.com/nation/current-affairs/060316/gowthampura-where-pele-is-god-brazil-is-heaven.html
[15] http://www.wifa.in/about/profilehistory/

like SS Narayanan, Fali Chinoy, Neville D'Souza, Joe D'Sa and Soli Poonawalla became quite famous in the Bombay circuit during this time.

Their next national title came in 1964, after having won a further two Santosh Trophies under the new name. In operation since 1937, the Tata Sports Club had to shut shop in 1980 when players chose professional clubs over industrial houses as they did not have to perform office duties, the typical 10-5 job after morning practice. Tata SC was a dominant force in Bombay, winning multiple Harwood Leagues. The furthest they went into the Rovers Cup was in 1974 when they lost to Dempo SC in the final. Since then, the downfall of fortunes hardly ceased and the famed name of Tata SC went into oblivion. Contemporary football in Mumbai saw a sharp decline in interest when clubs like Caltex, Mafatlal and Mahindra too decided to fold operations. Office clubs like Air India, ONGC remained but it was Mumbai FC that enjoyed a seven-season spell at the top in I-League before getting relegated in 2016–17.

However, the initial perk was inevitable, as Mahindra United had won the 2005–06 national leagues and also the Durand Cup, IFA Shield and the Federation Cup, twice. Mumbai City FC remains the only club in Mumbai currently either to play in I-League or the Indian Super League. The Ranbir Kapoor owned club has been actively trying to work at the grassroot levels to put Mumbai football back at the national level. The Islanders have gone to the Semi-Finals of the Indian Super League once.

GOA

The beautiful state of Goa was immersed deep into a five-hundred-year Portuguese colonisation. A Britisher, Reverend Father William Robert Lyons, brought the beautiful game to Goa in 1883.

Initially, arriving in Goa for the sun and sand in order to heal from his ailments, Fr Lyons never returned to Udipi, Mysore.

He set up a school in Siolim, Bardez, where he established sports as an important part of the curriculum, a thought so far-sighted which many schools still fail to deliver even in the twenty-first century. In 1893, the year football was declared as the national sport of Portugal, Antonio Francisco de Souza introduced it in a private English school in Salcete. This began the tradition of Christian missionary schools taking the game to the kids during their tender years—a perfect recipe for a bright future of the game alongside the Konkan coast. Hence, football became Goa's numero uno sport.

The Largo da Conceica at Panjim recorded the first ever match in 1900.[16] In attendance was the governor general of Goa. During the initial years of the twentieth Century, Panjim, Candolim, Mapusa, Margao and Assolna became hubs for budding players. Boys Social Club in Salcete, set up in 1905, was the first of its kind. St Mary's College, Bombay, paid a visit to Panjim Boys the same year. A British team became the first to take on Margao Boys at Largo dos Quarteis in Margao soon after. Interestingly, Goa hosted an international match in 1923 between British army officers and a team of Portuguese sports amateurs. The game won by the rulers of Goa gave birth to its very own tournament and Sporting Clube de Goa emerged champions in the game held at the Duler ground in North Goa. The Hindu Sporting Club from Mapusa organised the first All-Goa football tournament in 1930. By 1939, the Associacao de Futebol da India Portuguese (AFIP) was formed to structure the sport but it got dissolved within a decade.

A new dawn began with the emergence of the Major Faustino Duarte headed Conselho de Desportos da India Portuguese, a council administered by the government in 1951. Results showed as a two-tier league was introduced and Clube Desportivo Chinchinim were crowned inaugural champions of the Primeira Divisao. D Augusto de Noronha e Tavora, fondly known as Lube, the President

---

[16] Cyril Da Cunha, *Soccer in Goa* (Dept of Sports and Cultural Affairs 1978).

of Siolim Football Club was a great patron of the sport. He donated a trophy called the Taca Portugal and sponsored exchange trips for Goan teams to rub shoulders with teams from Bombay and adjoining areas. Teams from fellow Lusofonian nation Mozambique made a short trip in 1955, where they beat a select Goa XI 5-1. The administration of the game took a positive leap in 1959 when Lieutenant Joao Luis Aranha convinced the bankrupt Portuguese government to allow special dispensation to run football in Goa, also sanctioning the construction of numerous grounds, which would potentially serve as a source of revenue with the crowd hopefully paying to come see games in the stadium. The Associacao Futebol de Goa (AFG) was formed. The AFG was short-lived as the Portuguese left Goa in 1961. Goa lost its Iberian touch in a flash and it was left to the able hands of Lieutenant Aranha and Lube Tavora to help re-build the football structure with the help of Goa's first Chief Minister Dayananad Bandodkar. Bandodkar was a God-sent angel for most people in Goa. His love for the sport drove his determination towards scouting for talent, despite holding public office, not to mention the liberal spending behind the development of infrastructure of football within the state. The AFG transformed into the Goa Football Association (GFA), as it is known now. Within three years after its being successfully affiliated to the Western India Football Association (WIFA), Goa made its Santosh Trophy debut in 1964.[17]

Under the BM Parkkot administration, the GFA got affiliated to the All India Football Federation (AIFF) in 1968, and thus was born a great relationship of Goan greats in Indian football. The administrators grew impatient to showcase Goa's prowess on the national scene and the AIFF promised them the hosting rights of the 1972 Santosh Trophy contingent to them being able to host an All-India tournament first. In came the Bandodkar Trophy, named after the gold cup awarded by Chief Minister DB Bandodkar

---

[17] Nirmal Nath, *History of Indian Football* (Readers Service, 2011), pp. 47–54.

himself in 1970. At that point in time, the prize money was set at six lakh rupees, an astronomical figure seen for the first time in the country. Leaders Club of Punjab beat Salgaocar in the replayed final and the tournament left no doubts about Goa's capability to host the inter-state tournament. Although Goa did not win, football fever had gripped the coastal state like never before. However, there had been no clarity over a unified league in Goan regional football after the 1961 liberation.

The GFA introduced the Senior Division League in 1969–70 but was soon lost in time. Finally, the Super League came about in 1977–78 and Goa became the first state to go professional with its league beginning 1998–99. The Goa Pro League still runs strong even now. Youth football was spurred on quickly too and Goa became the U-19 champions in 1980 and 1983. Andrew D'Souza and Menino Figueredo became the first Goans in the national team. The first Santosh Trophy triumph came jointly with Bengal in 1983 when the replay remained goalless as well. Skipper Brahmanand Sankhwalkar came back the following year to deliver again as they beat Punjab in the final 1-0 in Madras. The likes of Sankhwalkar,[18] Derrick Pereira, Mauricio Afonso, Camilo Gonsalves became demi-gods in the state. More recently, clubs like Dempo SC, Sporting Clube de Goa, Salgaocar and Churchill Brothers have had varied successes in national competitions, keeping the Goan flag flying high. A total of five Santosh Trophy wins and a runners-up medal in the latest 2017 edition at home epitomises the love for football the people of Goa have.

There was some worry when spectatorship dwindled in NFL and I-League games but the introduction of the ISL and FC Goa's efforts to promote grassroots development, employing coaches and installing training facilities in each and every playground in the

---

[18] http://www.goaspider.com/resources/2266-football-Is-The-Most-Popular-Sport-Goa.aspx

state, provides a sense of a strong future for Goa, who always had been at par, if not better at its organisational structure than Bengal's IFA. Following Sporting Club de Goa, Salgaocar and Dempo standing out of the I-League, Churchill Brothers were reinstated into the I-League in the 2016–17 season. While the club finished second last in the league standing in 2017–18 they were left to face relegation due to relegation immunity being awarded to AIFF Youth Development programme Indian Arrows.

PUNJAB

Football in Punjab had its roots in present-day Pakistan in Lahore—the then capital of undivided Punjab. The King Edward Medical College had a deep ethos of producing talent and that trickled down to the formation of the North-West India Football Association in 1932. Punjab started playing in the Santosh Trophy since its inception in 1941, wherein in the first edition they had ten players of West Punjab Muslim origin, except one Sikh—Gurdeep Singh. Those times saw great players like Hafiz Rashid, Bachchi Khan, Jumma Khan, Kale Khan and Usman who formed the golden era of Kolkata's Mohammedan Sporting in the 1940s.

After the Partition and India's independence, the East Punjab Football Association was born in 1948[19] but the game in the state went unnoticed until the emergence of Jarnail Singh Dhillon—considered to be the greatest defender India had ever produced. The Kabbadi ground of Panam village is where Jarnail Singh had his roots. Excelling at both the sports, he was picked by the football team of Khalsa College, Mahilpur, and was called up to the Punjab XI and Khalsa Sporting Club followed by an offer from Kolkata's Rajasthan Club in 1957.

Two seasons later, Mohun Bagan came calling and the burly defender joined the 'Green and Maroon team' without any

---

[19] Nirmal Nath, *History of Indian Football* (Readers Service, 2011), pp. 100–108.

hesitation. He partnered with Chuni Goswami and Mohun Bagan steamrolled the1960s with numerous Calcutta Football League, Durand Cup and IFA Shields. His best moments on the field came in the 1962 Asian Games, winning gold and captaining the Asian All-Star XI in 1966 and 1967. The Ambala Heroes Club enjoyed a period of widespread success six decades ago winning more than thirty trophies under SD Chatterjee. In the 1956 Durand Cup, they defeated Mohun Bagan 2-0 in their opening match. Hence, Ambala, now in Haryana, became a small pocket in Punjab where football got immense popularity.

Another player, Inder Singh,[20] started making a name for himself as he joined another Punjab superpower Leaders Club, in 1962. The enigmatic forward also received call-ups to the Asian All-Star XI teams in the late 1960s. Leaders Club went on to surprise many and win the inaugural Bandodkar Gold Trophy in Goa, and in the meantime, football flourished as Punjab won the Santosh Trophy on home soil, beating Mysore 3-1 in the replayed final in 1970. The DCM Trophy allowed more Punjabi teams to showcase their talents, but sadly, that rang the death knell of Leaders Club. The Jagatjit Cotton and Textile Mills (JCT)[21] team foresaw a future and remained the only club in operation at the turn of the century from Punjab. Backed by industrialist Samir Thapar, a short tie-up with English side Wolverhampton Wanderers also saw the light of day. However, the club pulled out of the national league in 2010.

The Mahilpur Academy and the Minerva Academy of late have been churning out talents which have made it to the national team set-up. The only glimmer of hope in the I-League now remains the Minerva Punjab FC team. Minerva Punjab draws its

---

[20] www.jctfootball.com/aboutUs/famousPlayersProfile.aspx?ProfileCategoryID=6&ProfileID=2&OrderNumber=1

[21] http://www.thehardtackle.com/2010/jct-football-club-the-pride-of-punjab/

inspiration from Minerva Academy which has produced the highest number of officers for the Indian Armed Forces.

The 2017–18 I-League season saw Minerva script a fairytale, bringing the I-League trophy back to Punjab. Young husband-wife duo of Ranjit and Heena Bajaj took charge of the team combining their on-field and operational expertise to deliver Punjab's National League triumph after twenty-one years.

DELHI

The National Capital of India has had a bittersweet relation with the sport. The Delhi team won the second edition of the Santosh Trophy as hosts after finishing runners-up in the first. Delhi then was the hotbed of blue-ribbon tournaments—the Durand Cup, Subroto Mukherjee Cup and the DCM Trophy. The latter quickly lost steam but Subroto Mukherjee Cup[22] still remains the most prestigious All-India inter-school competition. New Delhi has also had the honour of hosting the oldest tournament in Asia and the third oldest in the world—Durand Cup.

The football culture was centred around the walled old city which supported football with all its fervour. With both the tournaments and club matches seeing fantastic audiences in Delhi, a strong connection was developed between the clubs and fans in the time close to the Indian independence. Clubs such as Mughals, Union, Young Men, New Delhi Heroes, Government Press, Crescent and Royal Air Force dominated the local scene. With quite a few players moving to Pakistan during that time, Delhi clubs continued visiting Pakistan to play games. As the city kept experiencing unprecedented growth, football in Delhi didn't keep pace with its glorious past, though the national tournaments continued to be supported fervently.

Delhi in a way can be credited for having produced probably one of the best players in the history of football in India. City FC's

---

[22] https://subrotocup.sportemis.com/

Sunil Chhetri joined Mohun Bagan as a teenager in 2002. The rest is history, as the striker is the highest international goalscorer for India, picking up stints in USA and Portugal in between.[23] The skipper of the Blue Tigers remains the face of Indian football at present. His 64 goals from 101 games for India, as on September 2018, remain the second highest by any active footballer in international football second only to Cristiano Ronaldo.

NORTH-EAST

When one speaks about the unexplored paradise of India—the North-East, football is easily one of the first few things which crops up and how rapidly it has made strides in the recent past. While cricket is the number one sport across the country, football definitely is the number one sport in the North-East of India.

An unmitigated Assam province, also consisting of the present day states of Meghalaya, Mizoram, Manipur and Nagaland saw football being played by the British in Guwahati and Jorhat, with the latter also having a league from 1911. Interestingly, the concept of a charity match was conceived here in the form of the Earle Cup in 1915, with the proceeds going to the Allied Forces in World War I. Tea plantation, oil drilling and the presence of aristocracy in Shillong Club, established in 1878, meant that football flourished under the English as the favourite pastime, alongside Polo, which is said to be invented by Manipur.

A year before independence, the Assam Football Association was formed and the Gauhati (now Guwahati)-based Maharana Club[24] drew critical acclaim through their performances in the 1939 IFC Shield in Lucknow and a draw twice with Mohammedan Sporting in the 1946 IFA Shield. Maharana Club produced the

---

[23] http://www.mlssoccer.com/news/article/wizards-sign-indian-forward-chhetri
[24] Subodh Malla Barua, Nirmal Nath, *History of Indian Football* (Readers Service, 2011), pp. 85–99.

best two players to come out of the state—Sarat Das and Talimeran Ao,[25] who went on to become the first captain of the independent Indian national football team in the 1948 London Olympics. Dr Ao, was a player and qualified physician who received his MBBS degree in 1950 from the Carmichael Medical College (now RG Kar Medical College) in Calcutta while playing for Mohun Bagan from 1943 to 1952. His leadership skills spoke volumes as he was also entrusted with the captaincy by the 'Green and Maroons' in 1948 and 1949. He was also part of the squad who never saw the light at the end of the tunnel in their quest to participate in the 1950 FIFA World Cup. Ao was posthumously awarded the Mohun Bagan Ratna in 2002, after a long struggle for deserved recognition.

The next major star from the region came long after, but became the poster boy in no time. Bhaichung Bhutia's goal from a bicycle kick against Border Security Force in the Durand Cup catapulted him to instant stardom—he was yet to be eighteen. Born in Tinkitam, Sikkim, Bhaichung was initiated into the national team quickly after his exploits at East Bengal and Head Coach Rustam Akhramov turned him into a striker extraordinaire. Trophies soon came as he joined JCT to win the inaugural 1996–97 National Football League, having a top score with fourteen goals. Kolkata welcomed him with open arms as he broke a seventy-year-old record in the Kolkata Derby, scoring a hat-trick against Mohun Bagan in a 4-1 win. At the end of the millennium, his decision to move to English second-division side Bury FC turned many heads. He continued to sizzle after he came back and ruled the Kolkata Maidans for years. Skippering the national side to a berth in the 2011 AFC Asian Cup, Bhutia retired as one of the most decorated players of the nation, with over a hundred senior caps and forty goals. He continues to remain involved, being part

---

[25] http://www.espn.in/football/story/_/id/17899572/doctor-pioneer-footballer-leader-remarkable-story-talimeren-ao

of various AIFF initiatives related to football and focusing on grassroots with his Bhaichung Bhutia Football Schools' academies. The North-East has been instrumental in the make-up of the national team squads in the recent past. The state of Sikkim, which only became a part of India in 1975 has produced two India captains—Pem Dorji, who became the first from the state to don national colours, and of course, Bhaichung. The Sikkim Football Association has also been hosting the All India Governor's Gold Cup since 1979 which has unearthed many talents from the hill-state. The All India Sir Churachandra Singh, KCSI, CBE Memorial tournament (CC Meet) has been going on in Manipur since the 1950s. It was only in 1973, that Manipur was officially recognised as an affiliate unit of the AIFF and thereon, football took a new turn as a host of talents migrated to Kolkata and the Tata Football Academy in Jamshedpur because of the lack of infrastructure within the state.

Somatai Shaiza was the first professional in the 1980s, followed by names like Gunabir Singh, Renedy Singh, Monitombi Singh, Tomba Singh and others. Tomba was the first Manipuri to be conferred the 'Best Footballer of the Year' by AIFF in 2003. That year the hosting of the National Games brought about the construction of the Khuman Lampak Sports Complex, the epicentre of football in the state now, and the football team went on to defy expectations, winning their maiden gold against four-time champs Kerala in the final. There has been no stopping ever since with fresh talents emerging. Names like Dhanachandra Singh, Gouramangi Singh, Jackichand, Konsham Chinglensana Singh have gone on to earn big contracts with ISL sides and have recently been joined by the young brigade from the India U-17 World Cup team like Dheeraj Moirangthem and Amarjit Khiyam.

While Assam, Manipur and Sikkim in the past have produced players, two states went the clubs route to excellence. Shillong and Meghalaya went from 'The Rock Capital of India' to be also known as the club capital of North-East India as Shillong Lajong became the first team to qualify for the I-League. A club formed in 1983 with the sole purpose of giving local youth a platform to perform, continued its journey of youth football and exporting players to the bigger teams until it one day saw itself standing on the cusp of representing the north-east football.

Mr P D Sawyan, the Chairman of Shillong Lajong, says, 'Lajong in Khasi means "our own" and that's exactly what the club was meant to be, a platform for our own players to be spotted, honed and presented. The club was also supposed to be the true pan north-eastern representative and not just one city or state.' Lajong saw their Shillong Premier League rivals Rangdajied qualify for I-League soon after and then entered another SPL rival, Royal Wahingdoh. Lajong still continues to play in the I-League.

Mizoram, on the other hand, has had a bumper success in recent times, all because of the modern approach towards how the game is organised and run—a structured league with professional teams, having a strong sense of youth development and an association that caters to the football crazy population of Mizoram. The Mizoram Premier League is now broadcasted in HD across the state by channels which are Mizo run and each match is played under lights with a sizeable fan attendance. Each one of Mizoram's youth teams has gone out and done well. Excellent coaches are always at hand to guide the young ones. It has come a long way from the stories of how Shylo Malsawmtluanga became the first Mizo player to sign a professional contract with East Bengal in 2002, to the state association signing a reported 1.25 crore deal,[26] to starting a domestic club league in 2012.

The emergence of Mizoram as a football powerhouse started with the state team winning the 2014 Santosh Trophy—its first ever and culminating in Aizawl FC winning the 2017 I-League.

---

[26] http://timesofindia.indiatimes.com/sports/football/top-stories/How-Mizoram-became-Indias-football-factory/articleshow/51185377.cms

Mohun Bagan squad that beat the East Yorkshire Regiment team to win the 1911 IFA Shield *(Credit: Wikipedia Commons)*
Disclaimer: This image is for representation purpose only.

Football is the No. 1 sport in North-East India. Fans at a Shillong Lajong game *(Credit: Shillong Lajong Media)*

Festivities at a Shillong Lajong game in Jawaharlal Nehru Stadium
(Credit: Shillong Lajong Media)

Bengaluru FC gave football fans a new lease of life in the city of Bangalore
(Credit: Bengaluru FC Media)

East Bengal fans before the Kolkata Derby against arch rivals Mohun Bagan *(Credit: AIFF Media)*

Bengaluru FC were the first Indian club to qualify for AFC Cup Final where they lost to Air Force Club of Iraq in 2016 *(Credit: Bengaluru FC Media)*

West Block Blues: Bengaluru FC's official fan club *(Credit: Bengaluru FC Media)*

Kingsley celebrates after scoring for Mohun Bagan against East Bengal in a 1-0 win in 2017/18 season *(Credit: AIFF Media)*

An intense battle between warriors of 2 clans in the middle of the pitch *(Credit: AIFF Media)*

The derby between East Bengal and Mohun Bagan is one of the most recognised and fiercest across the world *(Credit: AIFF Media)*

Newly formed Bengaluru FC were crowned the 2013/14 I-League Champions
(Credit: Bengaluru FC Media)

Miracle of Mizoram: Aizawl FC won the 2016/17 I-League title
(Credit: AIFF Media)

Minerva Punjab FC surprised everyone to take home the 2017/18 I-League Championship *(Credit: AIFF Media)*

India beat Tajikistan 4-1 in the AFC Challenge Cup 2008 to qualify for the AFC Asian Cup, Doha 2011 *(Credit: AIFF Media)*

India made it three titles in a row when they beat Syria in the Nehru Cup 2009 Final in Delhi *(Credit: AIFF Media)*

India after beating Cameroon in the final to lift the Nehru Cup for the fourth consecutive time. Delhi, 2011 *(Credit: AIFF Media)*

From lost in oblivion to giant slayers, this has been the story of football in the state, which is now the heartbeat of the game in India. Players like Jeje Lalpekhlua and Lalrindika Ralte have been top drawers for quite some time now. Youngsters like Daniel Lalhlimpuia, Jerry Lalrinzuala, Lalruathhara will make the future even safer.

Representation in leagues is not a far-fetched reality for north-eastern clubs anymore. Aizawl FC (Mizoram) has captured the imagination of millions, while NEROCA FC (Manipur) has made the step up recently by winning the national second division, following it up with a second place finish in season 2017–18. Not long ago, Royal Wahingdoh and Rangdajied United were playing out of Meghalaya and were the flag-bearers for the sport in the north-east. Shillong Lajong was the first club in the North-East to qualify for the I-League and is now the longest running I-League active participant after Mohun Bagan and East Bengal. United Sikkim FC,[27] under the patronage of Bhaichung Bhutia himself, made a brief appearance earlier in the I-League this decade. North-East United, which considers itself to represent each of the eight states, plays in the ISL, based out of Guwahati. It has attracted the attention of the football fans following the Indian Super League.

BACK TO BENGAL

The ball always rolled back into Kolkata, the epicentre from where it all began. Post the 1911 triumph, the royal rivalry was born, which had, has and will continue to define Indian football. The Mohun Bagan—East Bengal rivalry really escalated after Indian independence, even though their first reported meeting dates back to 1925. The 'Hindu Bengal' population who had to cross over to West Bengal in 1947 were plenty in numbers and a huge economic

---

[27] http://www.goal.com/en-india/news/1838/i-league-division-ii/2011/03/22/2406841/india-dazzling-launch-for-united-sikkim-as-bhaichung-bhutia

and social divide took place amongst them. The *Ghotis* were already residing there. For most of the immigrant people, East Bengal Club remained the only thread of reminiscence from their previous home which was then East Pakistan.

The sudden influx created a huge fight for space and identity, both physically and symbolically for the Bengalis in Kolkata. Football became the point of social supremacy and the first meeting itself after independence in the IFA Shield Final in 1947 had to be called off in the first time in lieu of crowd violence.[28] The police had to use teargas and fire twenty-two rounds to disperse the missile-clad crowd. This derby went on to create careers, end lives, bring tribulation and happiness—a mixed bag of a plethora of emotions which decorated the football enigma that was to be the city of Calcutta.

The story of how the 1975 IFA Shield final defeat of Mohun Bagan took the life of one Umakanto Palodhi[29] was spine-chilling, where he vowed in his suicide note, 'In my next birth, I will take revenge by becoming a Mohun Bagan footballer.' The 5-0 thrashing by East Bengal sent one of its own fans to the hospital suffering from a cardiac arrest due to sheer joy. Arguably the darkest hour of not only Indian football, but Indian sport in general was on 16 August 1980.

Sixteen lives were lost at the Eden Gardens, in another one of these Kolkata derbies as a result of a stampede which broke out in the high stands.[30] In 2012, forty people were injured as Mohun Bagan player Syed Rahim Nabi was hit by a stone,[31] flicked from the stands. The sentiments have remained strong and so have the

---

[28] Nirmal Nath, *History of Indian Football* (Readers Service, 2011), p. 316.
[29] http://www.goal.com/en-india/news/1064/i-league/2017/04/09/3737569/updated-11-facts-you-must-know-about-the-kolkata-derby
[30] http://www.goal.com/en-india/news/1064/i-league/2016/08/16/26560182/revisiting-16th-august-1980-the-darkest-day-in-the-history
[31] http://www.dailymail.co.uk/indiahome/indianews/article-2245507/Bloody-derbies-40-injured-Nabi-hit-stone-gallery.html

fierce clashes in the twenty-first century. The city's football landscape has seen better days and how! Pele arrived in the autumn of 1977 with his New York Cosmos. Eighty thousand people thronged the Eden Gardens to watch their very own Mohun Bagan rub shoulders with the 'King of Football'. The game ended 2-2 but left an indelible footprint in the minds of the Kolkata football fanatics. Kolkata has been the premier stopping point for a host of footballing icons over the years, be it Bobby Moore in 1984, or thousands welcoming Diego Maradona in 2008,[32] to Lionel Messi's Argentina playing a friendly against Venezuela in 2011.[33] Kolkata has had great success with football and its footballers. From producing legends like Sailen Manna, Chuni Goswami, the Banerjee brothers to making careers of almost each and every known footballer in Indian history, Kolkata has had its arms wide open without any discrimination, for the love of football.

---

[32] https://in.reuters.com/article/idINIndia-36904720081206
[33] http://www.goal.com/en-india/info/572/internationals/2011/08/31/1743699/lionel-messi-in-india-argentina-vs-venezuela-at-salt-lake

CHAPTER 4
FOOTBALL CLUBS OF INDIA

Football clubs or just 'clubs' as they are popularly known in football are essentially entities that keep the sport alive and kicking. Unlike any other sport which might have its own format and modes of competition, football has always thrived on clubs and the competition amongst the clubs within a constrained geographical boundary or outside. Football has been long known to have a strong and lasting impact on society and communities. This is precisely because clubs have been built on strong community lines. It adheres to the strong principle that people want to belong, people want to be part of something that is much more than an individual and stands for something more than what a single human being wants. Nothing fuels that desire more than football and clubs are usually the vehicle to do so.

This could even be a country divided by ideologies like Spain; Real Madrid is a club blessed by the royalty and Barcelona stands for the strong Catalan movement. Bilbao represents the Basque region. In his book *How Football Explains the World,* author Franklin Foer covers Barcelona in a chapter explaining the discreet charm of bourgeois nationalism. Foer writes that the motto of FC Barcelona is 'mas ques un club (more than a club)' and it, in fact, is more than just a club. The club presents a strong ideology to those who follow its football and the spillover is far larger than just limited to football.

Barcelona is the flag bearer of the Catalan identity and its politics. There is even a theory that the clubs colours, red and blue, are actually representatives of the French revolution. President of Catalonia, Jordi Pujol, has been said to recommend change of lineups, strategic formations and which players to recruit to the club management. The entire fabric of the Catalan area is firmly entrenched with 'more than a club' FC Barcelona. Clubs, like ideologies, do not die easily. Culture and community from where the clubs were born never allow it to. The carrier of this club like communication might change, but never dies.

In their book *Soccernomics,* authors Simon Kuper (a noted football author) and Stefan Syzmanzki (an Economics professor), talk about how in its entirety and for the time that football has run in England, only a few football clubs have been completely closed down. Not that football clubs are a great business—many suffer extreme losses, and this business which involves great dash of passion often sees clubs in the red. Many times, strong league rules relegate the club to the lower divisions. But at all times a strong community or the city bails the clubs out. Even at lower budgets or operational capabilities, clubs continue to be the torchbearers of the community.

Football clubs in India, much like anywhere else in the world, also came into being for a story, for a community coming together, for a message to reach across—for people to come together through the medium of their favourite sport. A sport that has a far closer bond to the people from all strata of life than any other sport could ever have.

Indian football club history is a long one, as explained in the previous chapters. However, club football in India came into prominence only after the institution of the cup competitions which were the playthings of the British in their early days. Major Indian football clubs were set off by the pioneering work done by a few clubs which are no longer around on the professional scene today.

MOHUN BAGAN

A lot of those early Indian clubs were formed in erstwhile Calcutta—the nerve centre of football in the country from the outset. Mohun Bagan was among the first native Indian clubs to be formed,[1] along with Town Club, Kumartuli Institute and Aryan Club. Bagan was founded in 1889, whereas the other three

---

[1] https://www.telegraphindia.com/1140710/jsp/opinion/story_18596803.jsp

were established between 1884 and 1886. While most associate Bagan with the entire city of Kolkata, the genesis of Bagan was in north Kolkata where three aristocratic Bengali families—Basu, Sen and Mitra—were instrumental in the formation of the Mohun Bagan Sporting Club on 15 August 1889.

Bhupendra Nath Basu—the first president of Bagan was a politician and activist—very actively involved in Indian nationalism. He was also the President of the Indian National Congress in 1914. Bagan was a vehicle to awaken nationalism and pride in the Bengali heart and to fuel the fire of independence to oppose the oppression of the British. Mohun Bagan was meant to bring Indians on an even keel with the ruling British on the football field and off it.

The first meeting of the club was presided over by Mr Basu himself, when he was just fourteen years old, at Balaram Ghosh Street in north Kolkata. Maharaja of Coochbehar and Shyam Pukur were reportedly in attendance at this meeting amongst many other people. Bagan was meant to be a tool to mobilise people together. The first ground of Mohun Bagan was at Marble Palace of the Mitra family—a ground which was reportedly not big enough for matches yet—where Bagan played their first game against the Eden Hindu Hostel.

Bagan won their first trophy in 1904—the Coochbehar Trophy. The new club secretary Subedar Major Salien Basu had a significant role to play in the club's history, and after his appointment in 1900, he laid huge importance on the physical training and fitness. Within a few years from 1904, Bagan had won the Gladstone Cup in 1905 beating Dalhousie 6-1 after winning the Coochbehar Trophy again. They won the Trades cup from 1906–08 consecutively three times. In 1906, they also won the Minto Fort Trophy which was the second most prestigious trophy after the IFA shield. 1909 saw Bagan winning the Laxmibilash Trophy as well.

Bagan's practice ground story is fascinating as well. While their first ground was Marble Palace, from 1900 onwards they started sharing the Kolkata Ground (Maidan) with Presidency College. This continued till 1905, post which they moved to the National AC ground which they continued using till 1963.

IFA shield was the most prestigious tournament in those days and only a few Indian clubs who dreamt of playing in the tournament saw reality. Bagan along with four other teams—Shovabazar, Townclub, Heir Sporting and Chinsurah Sporting—saw this reality in 1909. The club made a quick exit from the tournament but that was only a precursor to what they were going to achieve in the next IFA Shield.

In 1911, Bagan scripted the most historic moment yet in Indian football. The 1911 IFA Shield saw Bagan beat St Xavier and Rangers 3-0 in the first round and second round respectively, and then Rifle brigade by 1-0 in the third round. Middlesex Regiment was beaten in the Semi-finals by Bagan 3-1 in the second day replay. It set up an exciting Finals clash against the East Yorkshire Regiment. Attended by 80,000 spectators who could not really witness the match since there were no stands, the spectators relied on the information which was passed on by those who had ringside seats to the game.

In a fifty-minute game separated by a five-minute break, Bagan lost the toss. East Yorkshire was placed on the Fort William side and Bagan on the Eden Garden side. Thus, under referee HG Puller began the historic game on 29 July 1911 between Bagan and East Yorkshire regiment. Bagan were led by mercurial forward Shibdas Bhaduri while East Yorkshire was led by Sergeant Jackson. Bagan began the first half on the front aggressively seeking all important goals. Bagan's attacking troika of Bijoydas Bhaduri, Kanu Roy and Shibdas Bhaduri kept the East Yorkshire defenders on their toes. East Yorkshire had their chances as well. The first half ended on an even keel and East Yorkshire made a strong start coming back from the break with Sergeant Jackson scoring all important goals. But this was Bagan's day—a day to be marked in the history of Indian football. Shibdas Bhaduri quickly evened the score, scoring soon after and right around the time that the game was to end. He passed to Abhilash Ghosh, who neatly tucked the ball to mark an important event for Indian football.

Mohun Bagan who was now an Athletic Club and not a Sporting Club had won the 1911 IFA shield beating the mighty East Yorkshire regiment, playing football barefoot. The glass ceiling of football in India was broken in that moment.

The event garnered huge interest in the media, both in Bengal and back in the UK. Noticing the victory, *The Manchester Guardian* wrote, 'The team comprising Bengalis won the IFA shield beating three top Military teams. 80,000 Indians will remain witness to this event. There is nothing to be surprised at. The team that is fit, has sharp surveillance and intelligence, wins.' *The Bengali* sang praises by publishing a poem in honour of Bagan on 30 July.

> *Thanks my friends of football renown*
> *For bringing the British teams down.*
> *A victory grand to behold,*
> *Serene and noble—bright and bold—The Mohun Bagans.*

Even the Moslem Football Club supported their Hindu brothers' victory over the British. A victory for one football club was victory for the entire country, state, community and society. Football is, and has always been, firmly entrenched in the communities.

The 1920s saw Bagan being invited to the Rover's Cup in Mumbai and it became the first ever Indian team to feature in the Durand Cup. They lost their long-standing president Bhupendranath Basu and he was replaced by Rajendranath Mukherjee. Subedar Major Salien Basu also expired in the beginning of 1931 and Mohun Bagan AC lost their two biggest patrons. In 1911, the hero Shibdas Bhaduri also passed away. Bagan celebrated their diamond jubilee in 1949 having invited Swedish team Helsingberg for a tri-match series.

In the celebrations that took place, the then Chief Minister of Bengal Bidhan Chandra Roy mentioned that during the freedom struggle of the country Mohun Bagan inspired the youth of Bengal. In 1951, Asian Games saw four Mohun Bagan players making it to the Indian football team—Sailen Manna, T Aao, Abhay Ghosh and Runu Guhathakurta. Sailen Manna led team won the gold beating the then powerhouse Iran 2-0 in the Finals. When Bagan won the 1952 Durand Cup beating the National Defence Academy, Dehradun, the chief guest, Honourable President Dr Rajendra Prasad, spoke of his fondness for the club and how as a student in Kolkata he had attended all the matches of the club.

Bagan followed up by winning the Rovers Cup for the first time in 1956. Bagan legend Chunni Goswami was then coming to the fore as one of the best players in the country leading the Bagan charge. Trophies, titles and various tournaments kept trickling in as Bagan led the charge, decade after decade, firming up its claim as one of the biggest clubs in India.

The 'Maroon and Greens' moved into the National Football League and I-League era, being one of the most successful Indian clubs having four titles and four runners-up. Their rivalry with East Bengal had become legendary and attracted attention from football fans from all across the world.

MOHAMMEDAN SPORTING

Mohammedan Sporting had a fair number of name changes before it finally came into being as Mohammedan Sporting in 1891. It tracks its origin to 'Jubilee Club' formed in Kolkata in 1887 by Nawab Aminul Islam. The name was changed to Crescent Club and then to Hamidia Club before it finally came to be known as Mohammedan Sporting in 1891.[2]

While the other two prominent clubs were divided by Bengali identity, Mohammedan's identity was related to Bengali

---

[2] https://en.wikipedia.org/wiki/Mohammedan_S.C._(Kolkata)

Muslims and was again primarily a voice against the British. Mohammedan Sporting were the flag bearers of the Indian Muslim nationalist movement. Its current status as I-Leagues Second Division club does not do the club justice as the club has had a glorious past that includes many firsts in Indian football. They were the first team to win the Durand Cup in 1940, the first Indian team to win a tournament on foreign soil (The Aga Khan Gold Cup in Dhaka in 1960), the first club to win the Calcutta Football League, the first club to win the prestigious Calcutta Football League five years in a row from 1934–38 and the first club to do a League and IFA Shield double in 1936.

The 1940s Durand Cup Final where the club faced Royal Warwickshire Regiment was in some ways similar to the 1911 Bagan-East Yorkshire regiment game. A hundred thousand people had gathered at the Irwin Amphitheater—a place where the current day National Stadium exists—on 12 December 1940.[3] The game saw huge interest from Muslims across India as they saw Mohammedan Sporting as the beacon of Indian Muslim Nationalism. Politicians and commoners alike came together for the game, marked also for being the first Final game that an Indian official took charge of.

Major Harnam Singh officiated the game, which the two British linesmen agreed to, on being threatened of getting a court martial by the Viceroy of India, Lord Linlithgow. Centre forward Hafiz Rashid and Saboo scored in this remarkable victory of eleven Muslim players against the British team. The story has become folklore in the walled part of the city of Delhi.

Much of Mohammedan Sporting's success also was due to the fact that they scouted players from far and wide, not limited to a particular region.

Muslims from across India identified with the club and owing to a massive base of supporters, the players were hired from different

---

[3] https://qz.com/286516/how-its-glorious-past-is-linked-to-the-uncertain-future-of-mohammedan-sporting/

parts of India. Jumma Khan, Bachi Khan and Saboo came in from North-West Frontier Province (now in Pakistan), Forwards, Rahmat and Midfielder Mohiuddin joined in from Bengaluru. Anwar came in from Quetta and captained the side for a long time. Rahim came from Hyderabad and Goalkeeper Usman Jan was recruited from Crescent Club in Delhi. Legend Sailen Manna called Usman the best Goalkeeper ever seen by him.

In 1948, Mohammedan Sporting was the first side to win the Calcutta Football League post-independence. In an atmosphere that was still laced with partition movement, Mohammedan won the league and CFL was lauded for fairness of conduct. Mohammedan also changed its policy and recruited players from all religions. Any appearance by Mohammedan Sporting at the Ambedkar Stadium still ensures a packed house as was the case a couple of seasons back when they won the Durand Cup 2013.

EAST BENGAL

The third of the Kolkata big three—East Bengal—was formed only in 1921. The story of East Bengal, Mohammedan Sporting and Mohun Bagan is a true representative of the football's entrenchment in communities. East Bengal's existence came out of a game between Mohun Bagan and Jorabagan on 28 July 1920 playing each other in a Coochbehar Trophy tie. Jorabagan took the field without their star defender Sailesh Bose, whose exclusion was mysterious. Jorabagan club's vice president and industrialist Suresh Chandra Chaudhuri pleaded for Bose's inclusion with the club authorities but it fell on deaf ears. A visibly annoyed Chaudhuri immediately severed all connections with Jorabagan, left the ground and took with him Tarit Bhusan Roy, Raja Manmatha Nath Roy Chaudhuri, Ramesh Chandra Sen and Aurobindo Ghosh.

In a meeting at Kripanath Building, Sovabazaar, the new club established on 1 August 1920 was christened East Bengal. Since the founders were from the eastern part of Bengal (modern day Bangladesh) it was called East Bengal. Raja Manmatha Nath

Chaudhari was the Raja of Santosh which is now in Bangladesh. Indian State Football Championship—Santosh Trophy—has been named after him.

Clubs' colours were a little tough to arrive at but that problem was also sorted out soon after the founders saw a red and gold shirt hanging at Whiteaway, Laidlaw & Co Departmental Store at Chowringhee. The club crest also has a nationalistic story behind it. Struck by the Satyagraha wave in 1930, clubs in Calcutta refused to participate in the Calcutta Football League midway through the season. While Royal Regiment was declared the winner, East Bengal was not promoted to first division. Angered by this decision, the supporters decided to hold a protest march at the East Bengal grounds holding flaming torches. Thus, the club crest originated from the idea of the *mashal*. One of the most successful football clubs in the country, East Bengal has won the National Football League title three times and currently are on an eight season winning run in the Calcutta Football League. They won their thirty-ninth CFL in the 2017 season under new coach and I-League champion Khalid Jamil.

Participating in the 2003 ASEAN Cup, East Bengal won the tournament beating Thailand powerhouse BEC Tero Sasana in the Finals. BEC had beaten East Bengal 1-0 in the group and only a strong performance against Philippine Army got East Bengal through to the knockout stages. Two strong performances against local Indonesian clubs Persita Tangerang and Petrokimia Putra put East Bengal in the Finals. Sikkim Sniper Bhaichung Bhutia was in fine form in the tournament as buoyed by his goals, East Bengal won the Championship beating BEC in the Finals. Bhaichung got the maximum number of goals and Sandip Nandy, who didn't expect he would get any game-time, was adjudged the best goalkeeper of the tournament. Subhas Bhowmick was the coach and Suley Musah the captain of the team. Featured along with East Bengal stalwarts such as Alvito D'Cunha and Deepak Mandal, they were greeted at Kolkata airport by a massive gathering of East Bengal fans as the cup win had created quite a stir back home.

The geographical, ideological, philosophical and communal division of Bengal happened through football. Mohun Bagan AC today represents what are called native Kolkata Bengalis; East Bengal by their name represent Hindu migrants from Bangladesh while Mohammedan Sporting captured the imagination of the Muslims from Bengal.

Although there are records as early as the 1830s to the 1880s of football being played between the clubs—mostly between British regimental and infantry outfits—the advent of the Durand Cup in 1888 started off the club football culture in Indian football. Soon after, the IFA Shield followed in Calcutta. While the Durand Cup in Shimla and the IFA Shield in Calcutta showed where the power centre of Indian football lay, another competition, now defunct, in India's western belt was sandwiched between the two oldest active football tournaments in the country.

The Rovers Cup was established in 1891 in Bombay (now Mumbai) and was also the brainchild and safe haven of the British, considering the fact that only in 1923 the first Indian club was invited to participate in the tournament—Mohun Bagan. However, Indian clubs soon put their feet on the pedal and their rise in prominence, as the British Empire in India was fading in the twentieth century, is a perfect way to explain the Indian society which was slowly freeing itself from the clutches of colonialism. The birth and rise of the football clubs in Kolkata was an important tipping point in Indian history, sports notwithstanding. However, it was Mohun Bagan's 1911 IFA Shield win at a time when the power base of the empire was shifting from Calcutta to Delhi that became a strong symbol of the power of Indians over their colonial rulers. Mohammedan Sporting's success spree in the 1930s even witnessed one of their star players, Mohammed Salim, head to Celtic in Scotland only for the player to return homesick.

For an Indian footballer to play abroad was never thought of as a possibility, but if that was not a sign of the things to come, then what was? It was not only in Bengal that the influence of Kolkata's big three was spreading. For example, Mohammedan's religious connotations brought together Muslims across India to cheer for a common team. Calcutta was the nerve centre of British India. Kolkata's strong club culture led to a lot of promising clubs from the city springing up to get counted on the national football scene. Most prominent amongst them have been United SC who have had some impressive time in the I-League. Southern Samity, Tollygunje Agragami, Peerless, Bhawanipore, George Telegraph—all have contributed to the Indian football scenario.

ATLETICO DE KOLKATA (ATK)

An ambitious project that was launched by a consortium of five partners—cricketer Sourav Ganguly, businessmen Sanjiv Goenka, Harshvardhan Neotia, Utsav Parekh and Spanish football giants Atletico De Madrid—won the bid for the Indian Super League Kolkata franchise. A consortium which presented such a strong face that they were believed to have won the bid over Shahrukh Khan's KKR franchise.

In a city steeped in history of football and established legacy of the clubs, ATK has established itself as a strong candidate to compete in the times to come. Their trophy cabinet already ranks them as the most successful club in the Indian Super League alongside Chennaiyin FC. Fuelled by the technical expertise of the Atletico Madrid, ATK has won the ISL twice on the back of some superb performances on the pitch by a great mix of Indian and international players. Atletico Madrid has since exited the tie-up with Mr Goenka having bought his stake out. Former Manchester United legend, Teddy Sherringham, took over the reins at the club as their Coach in 2017–18 season with former Bengaluru FC Head Coach Ashley Westwood brought in as the technical director.

Former Republic of Ireland, Tottenham Hotspurs and Liverpool Striker Robbie Keane donned the captain's armband for the 2017–18 Indian Super League season. The season became one to be forgotten because Teddy Sherringham was asked to leave midway through the league, with Ashley Westwood taking over in the interim before vacating the post at the end of the season. Robbie Keane suffered from injuries, yet managed to secure eight goals in eleven games in the Indian Super League and Super Cup. He was also the designated manager of the club after Teddy Sherringham was asked to leave. The team finished a lowly ninth which was the club's lowest ever finish.

A fresh approach has been taken ahead of the 2018–19 season by bringing in experienced ISL manager Steve Coppell to helm the season.

GOAN POWERHOUSE CLUBS

In Goa, as was the case in Kolkata, British missionaries took to the task of popularising football and, as early as 1905, the first Goan club was established called the Boys Social Club.[4] However, Goan football clubs only came to prominence after India's independence in the mid-twentieth century. Goan clubs Vasco, Salgaocar, Dempo were the first established big teams in the state. Although club football in Goa as part of the Goa First Division started way back in 1951, Goan clubs came into national prominence only during the successful days of Dempo, Salgaocar, Sporting Club De Goa and Churchill Brothers in the National Football League and the I-League.

However, turn of events have seen the big Goan clubs pull out of top division football in recent years. In the 2016–17 season, only two Goan clubs—FC Goa, formed in 2014, and Churchill Brothers, formed in 1988—were the state's only representatives in the ISL and the I-League respectively. 2017–18 season saw Churchill Brothers being relegated to finishing second last

---

[4] http://forcagoa.org/where-it-started/history-of-football/

only ahead of Indian Arrows who have relegation immunity. Churchill Brothers have applied for reversal of the relegation with the AIFF.

DEMPO SC

One of the most successful clubs in Indian club history, Dempo SC, between 2005 and 2012 had won five National League titles—two in the National Football League days and three since I-League was introduced. Owned by the Dempo family, Dempo SC started off as the Dempo Souza Football Club in 1968 and has gone on to become the most successful football club in the country. While Dempo were relegated in the 2014–15 season they qualified for the I-League in 2015–16 by virtue of winning the I-League 2.

However, the club, along with two other Goan clubs Salgaocar and Sporting Club De Goa, decided to withdraw from the league. Nicknamed the 'golden eagles', Dempo was indeed a golden club for Goa as under manager Armando Colaco a golden generation of players dominated Indian football in the National Football League and early years of I-League. Mahesh Gawli, Samir Naik, Clifford Miranda, Climax Lawrence, Beto and Ranti Martins were a golden generation of Dempo players who dominated the Indian domestic football scene winning one trophy after another.

CHURCHIL BROTHERS

Founded in 1988 as Varca Club before changing their name to Brothers Sporting Club and then to Churchill Brothers after being bought over by Churchill Alemao, two I-League titles amongst countless other wins saw Churchill dominate the football headlines of the state and India.

Churchill was barred from playing in the I-League after having failed the AFC Club Licensing. A legal battle followed with the club winning the case against the national federation to be reinstated in the 2016–17 edition of the I-League. It is currently the only club from Goa to be playing in the I-League as three other illustrious clubs have decided not to be involved in the sport on the National League level.

SALGAOCAR SC

The oldest of the Goan teams was founded in 1956 by the VM Salgaocar group of companies. The club is currently owned by his son Shivanand Salgaocar. The club became the first Goan club which was extended the invitation of playing in the Durand Cup in 1962.

Against the background of Goa's integration with the nation in 1961, Prime Minister Pt Jawaharlal Nehru was so happy with Salgaocar's participation in the tournament in Delhi that he hosted the team at his residence. Nineteen Goa Pro-League titles and two national titles came Salgaocar's way as they marked their presence on the Indian domestic scene.

SPORTING CLUB DE GOA

In 1999, people of Panjim decided to launch a football club after Cidade de Goa disbanded its football team. It was called Sporting Club de Goa inspired by the famous Sporting Club de Portugal.

Sporting became the second club of public shareholding in Goa after Vasco. It shot to prominence in the 2001–02 Federation Cup, after making it to the top four there. They made their NFL debut in 2003–04 and were on the verge of winning their first league championship but lost out on the last day of the season to Dempo. The season saw a horrific bus accident which ruled out four of their players for the season and left many others injured. Dudu Omagbemi, after firing on all cylinders, managed to compete strongly and heroically came second ahead of East Bengal, Mohun Bagan and Mahindra United.

FC GOA

The Indian Super League chose a consortium consisting of Videocon Industries, Dattaraj Salgaocar, Dempo SC (through principal owner Srinivas Dempo) for the Goa franchise in the Indian Super League. Current Indian cricket captain Virat Kohli was roped in as an owner later. Brazilian Legend Zico was at the helm of affairs as FC Goa began their trip in the Indian Super League.

Playing out of the Fatorda stadium in Margao, Goa began badly in the 2014 season. However, buoyed by an excellent leader in Zico they came back strongly to qualify for the Semi-finals where they were eventually beaten by Atletico de Kolkata. The next season saw a resurgent Goa which dominated the tournament on their way to the Finals of the event where they squared off against an in-form Chennaiyin. Leading the final 2-1, Goa let the lead slip and lost the game 3-2.

In the aftermath of heated discussions among the two parties post the game, owners Dattaraj Salgaocar and Srinivas Dempo offloaded their stake to the Deltin group which became the principal owners of the clubs. 2016 season brought no respite to FC Goa as they struggled with injuries and finished last. Zico, who was the only coach in the Indian Super League along with Marco Materazzi to have been at the helm of affairs for three seasons, resigned.

Goan legend Derrick Pereira was brought in as the Assistant Coach and director of youth to lead the revival of the club along with former Barcelona Youth Team Coach Sergio Lobera. With a strong core of Goan players backed by Spanish-Moroccan combined foreign line-up, Goa again marched on to the Semi-finals losing out to eventual champions Chennaiyin. Ferran Corominas became the highest goalscorer in 2017–18 scoring an all-time high of eighteen goals in one season.

While Goa amongst other city-based teams is considered as a one-unit place, it is worth noting that almost all teams who are or have played on the national front are from different cities in Goa. While Vasco is the headquarters of Salgaocar, Panjim is the Sporting Club de Goa and Dempo SC's home. Churchill Brothers are predominantly Margao based while FC Goa plays at the Fatorda in Margao too. Goa has, in recent times, seen its clubs struggle for buoyancy in the football ecosystem. It would require all the support to bring back Goa to its days of glory, which in turn would help India.

KERALA

While football partisanship was in full swing in Kolkata and Goa, another hotbed of Indian football—Kerala—was emerging. The Kerala Football Association joined the AIFF in 1957 and club football in Kerala caught the fancy of the state's massive number of football fans. The first big club teams from Kerala were the Malabar District Football Association (MDFA) XI and Kerala Police. That said, Kerala football only came into general prominence in the late twentieth century leading up and into the twenty-first century.

FC Kochin became the first professional football club in India and soon roped in star local players like IM Vijayan and Jo-Paul Ancheri to become the talk of Indian football but its time at the top proved to be short-lived. Less than ten years after being formed in 1997, FC Kochin was consigned to Indian football's periphery which was a big blow to Kerala football. While the local football scene in the state thrived due to the unending passion for the game of the locals and the host of local tournaments that were held, there was barely participation from the state at the national level.

Viva Kerala was another club from Kerala that threatened to upset the national status quo, but it was a bridge too far as Viva Kerala also faded into oblivion for want of funding and big sponsorships. It ended up folding midway through I-League's short history, leaving the bigwigs from Kolkata and Goa to once again remain the top clubs in Indian football until the advent of the North-East brigade, Bengaluru FC and the ISL.

Despite the emotional and passionate connection of the state of Kerala with football, the sport's introduction to the state on a wider scale only came about after the 1950s.

KERALA BLASTERS FC

If there was one stadium one would like to visit to get a feel of how exciting a game of football can be in India—Kerala Blasters home game should definitely be the number two on that list. Number two only because the Mohun Bagan-East Bengal derby is probably the best football game which fans get to see.

Blasters have done decently well and the fact that it is owned by the cricket legend Sachin Tendulkar is an added bonus for anyone going to the game. Football loving Kerala did not really see too much elite league action for a long time before Kerala Blasters was awarded to Prasad V Potlouri and Sachin Tendulkar. The team extended hands and now the team is owned by N Prasad, Sachin Tendulkar and filmstars—Nagarjuna, Chiranjeevi and Allu Arvind.

The Kochi crowd did turn up in large numbers to support their team as sixty thousand wild, crazy, shouting fans gathered in the stadium each match day when David James led Blasters made it to the Finals in the inaugural season in 2014. Had it not been for a wonder save by ATK Goalkeeper Edel Bete, denying British born, Indian origin Striker, Michael Chopra, Kerala could very well have been the first champions of the Indian Super League.

The third season saw Steve Coppell taking charge of a side that started slow but eventually gained steam and marched on to the Finals losing only on penalties to ATK again. Former Manchester United Assistant Coach Rene Meulensteen took over the club ahead of 2017–18 and brought in Manchester United old boys Dmitar Berbatov and Wes Brown. The season again didn't pan out as expected and midway through the league, Kerala Blasters called up their old manager David James—a move that probably proved to be too late, as despite a good run of form the team finished sixth in the season. David James was handed the reins of the club for two further seasons ahead of the 2017–18 season.

ISL's best supported club also hosted the La Liga World Trophy in July-August 2018 with La Liga team Girona travelling to Kochi along with A League side Melbourne City FC. Kerala Blasters has become an exceptionally strong brand recognised not just across India but the world with the support that the team receives. Their fan club Manjapadda Kerala Blasters FC has been one of the most vocal fan's groups seen in India. It has garnered a lot of attention from across the world as well.

MAHARASHTRA

In contrast, one of India's biggest states—Maharashtra—already had a thriving football culture since the early 1900s but the lack of a football fan base, in conjunction with the state being the cricketing nerve centre of India, meant that football in Maharashtra did not reach the levels of Kolkata or Goa. Mumbai, which was the nerve centre of football in Maharashtra, became the cricket capital of India and emergence of Kolhapur as a strong football pocket was only miniscule.

That said, a few clubs like Mahindra & Mahindra, Air India, Bharat FC, ONGC Pune FC, Mumbai FC and the more recently DSK Shivajians, ISL clubs FC Pune City and Mumbai City FC have ensured the representation of the state of Maharashtra in the top level of Indian football. Despite being perhaps the biggest financial centre in India and being led by possibly one of the most active state federations in Western India Football Association, Maharashtra audiences have not really warmed up to the idea of football viewing in the same fashion as they have made Mumbai the capital of Indian cricket.

Maharashtra's two strong cities, Pune and Mumbai, have both seen clubs come in and put up a great professional front which till Bengaluru FC's advent onto the Indian scene was not witnessed elsewhere.

PUNE FC

Ashok Piramal Group's foray into football was marked by Pune FC coming as a football club from the city of the same name. It was the first time that the new age metropolitan city Pune, with its ever increasing student population, had a football club of this scale. It was indeed a breath of fresh air for football fans to see a professional set up like Pune which laid great emphasis on the youth football system in the city and also worked towards garnering fans and communities from within the city.

In its second attempt in the I-League 2, the club qualified for the I-League and played the I-League 1 in 2009–10. Their first season saw them finish third in the league and they also announced an academy in 2011 making them the first club with a full-fledged academy team. The club played English side Blackburn Rovers in 2011 before going on and giving their best in 2012 finishing second in the season. The club's increased focus on youth was refreshing and became the hallmark of a truly new age club coming to India.

Chirag Tanna, who was leading the project at that point of time in an interview said, 'We had decided on it (setting up a youth academy) from the day the club was formed and we looked into having an all-residential academy later.' Possibly the only problem that the club faced initially was the fact that Pune was not really braced up to football in a manner Kolhapur would have been, and while the city did have a huge population of young students not many would make the journey to Balewadi Sports Complex on the outskirts of the city to watch the game. The club eventually pulled out of the I-League before the 2015–16 season. The well-set-up Pune FC youth academy was taken over by ISL Franchise FC Pune City.

2014–15 season saw the entry of another football club from Pune. Kalyani Bharat FC was introduced to the city as the second team after Pune FC. Bharat FC was again a well organised club set up with similar fundamentals to that of Pune FC, with an aim to focus on youth development and working towards making Pune a strong football city. A well assembled squad however failed to deliver, resulting in the team folding up at the end of the season. The next season saw an old club Shivajians who had been taken up by a business house DSK and had competed in the second division earlier to take up the franchise spot available and play the I-League.

DSK had a very established infrastructure and youth development structure through their tie up with English Premier League Club Liverpool. They had been consistently playing the youth I-League and were on their way to play the I-League 2 when their bid to play in the I-League was approved. Derrick Pereira, who had taken over as the technical director for the club then, had to don the Head Coach cap and lead the team to the I-League with little or no time to prepare. Results were not great, and while the team went on a decent unbeaten run towards the end of the campaign they finished last saved only by the relegation immunity provided to franchise teams.

Another season under English Coach Dave Rodgers only brought slight betterment of the record. Certain financial conditions at the promoters end forced DSK Shivajians to pull out of the I-Legaue 2017–18 while the academy continues to run.

FC PUNE CITY

FC Pune City was started in 2014 as a result of Indian Super League bid won by the Wadhawan group along with Bollywood star Hrithik Roshan and Italian Serie A side Fiorentina were added to the list of owners after the bid allotment. In the first three seasons of the Indian Super League, FC Pune City had put together a very strong side but had failed to reach the Final 4 of the tournament—a record they set right in Season 4 of the Indian Super League.

A fine mix of youth players coupled with experienced ISL foreigners like 2016 top goalscorer Marcelinho, Emiliano Alfaro, Marcos Tebar saw FC Pune City qualify for the Final 4 of the Indian Super League 2017–18.

They have greatly focussed on the development of youth after taking over Pune FC's Academy and by having their own women's football team. The different age group teams of FC Pune City and their women's team have won a lot of tournaments across India and to a certain extent they have been the pioneers of branching out of the first team operations amongst the India Super League sides.

NORTH-EAST INDIA

While clubs from Kolkata, Goa, Kerala and other hotbeds of Indian football have been dominant forces of Indian football, the 2016–17 champions of India's top two divisions—the I-League and the second Division I-League—were from north-east India.

Mizoram's Aizawl FC won the I-League 2016–17 and Manipur's NEROCA FC won the second Division I-League 2016–17. NEROCA followed that up with a second placed finish in the 2017–18 I-League season. In fact, in each of the last eight seasons of I-League barring two, a team from the north-east has won promotion to the I-League. I-League 2017–18 featured as many as three teams from the north-east amongst the mix— each one of them was from a different state in the north-east of India. The players from north-east have been representing India and playing for big Kolkata and Goa clubs long before Aizawl and NEROCA's success.

SHILLONG LAJONG

While it was a known fact that players from the north-east grew up in a strong culture of football and were gifted with outstanding physical abilities, not many teams from the north-east believed in testing their mettle on the India stage. This glass ceiling was broken by the pioneer of the sport—Shillong Lajong.

The Meghalaya-based Shillong Lajong gained historic entry into the I-League in 2009, becoming the first club from the northeast to play in India's top flight. The team suffered instant relegation and trial by fire before making a strong comeback to the I-League. Lajong's gamble to only play north-east players in their squad has paid off big time as not only have the local fans attached their affinity to the team but the whole of north-east now looks forward to having their players play for the Reds. 'We might currently be the Bilbao of Indian football but we have our aspirations some day to be the Barcelona,' … Lajong's Managing Director Larsing Ming Sawyan, also an AIFF Vice President, told FIFA's Futbol Mundial few years ago.

Lajong's story is an extremely interesting one. Shillong Lajong Football Club was formed in 1983 by two gentlemen—Kitdor Syiem and Prabhat Dey Sawyan. After yet another disappointing Meghalaya Invitation Cup for the local teams in 1982, where no local football club could advance into the final stages, these two decided to have their own club to promote local talent and inculcate a sense of pride amongst the local fans who were at times seen cheering for outstation teams scoring against the local teams. Thus, Lajong Sports Social and Cultural Club (Lajong means 'our own' in Khasi) was born in 1983, with the sole aim of promoting local football talent and a belief that the region had no dearth of good footballers.

Prabhat Dey Sawyan, chairman of Shillong Lajong reflected on the event, 'Early 1980s was a time of turbulence and turmoil in the north-eastern region of India and Shillong was reeling under the ill-effects of the prevailing socio-political climate. People, particularly the youth, were confused and in a state of utter bewilderment and anguish, searching for answers. Football, a passion, almost a religion for the people had plummeted to the lowest standards ever and spectators and supporters were distraught at the extremely poor performance of the local teams in the regional and national tournaments. It dawned upon us that the search for answers was inside and within us, and therefore, what better way to revitalise and rejuvenate our spirits than to strive and "score our own goals". So the Lajong was born as a vehicle to generate positive energy and development by inculcating a spirit of "Inner Self Confidence".'

Sikkim United spearheaded by Indian football's golden boy Bhaichung Bhutia joined Lajong soon in the I-League. The trend has continued in the ensuing years, and NEROCA's promotion to the I-League in the coming season will make it the first club from the talent-rich state of Manipur to feature in the top division.

Clubs like Royal Wahingdoh, Rangdajied United and Aizawl had followed Shillong Lajong's lead to the I-League. Most northeast clubs have always been the nursery for the bigger clubs but 2016–17 was the watershed season as a young Lajong squad, with an average age of twenty-one, finished fifth in the I-League with Mizoram's Aizawl FC completing a Leicester story in India by winning the I-League in a remarkable fashion beating the more fancied Mohun Bagan, East Bengal and Bengaluru FC to the title.

AIZAWL FC

Former Indian International Khalid Jamil fashioned a remarkable title win in the 2016–17 season. Aizawl embraced a lifeline thrown their way by the All India Football Federation by reinstating them in the I-League despite having been relegated the previous season by pulling off possibly the biggest upset in the history of Indian football by going on to win the I-League. Syrian Midfielder Mahmoud Al Amna, who had previously played for Goan outfit Sporting Club De Goa, was the star performer in a team that collectively put together a very organised front. Game after game, Aizawl continued defying odds and ended up lifting the prestigious trophy. Owner Robert Royte harbours an all Mizo Aizawl FC champion dream though. It is not tough to figure out why Mizoram has been at the forefront of development of the sport in India and why Aizawl have been the champions of India.

Royte mentions, 'Mizoram always had players, but the focus on infrastructure development and youth development programmes has given the game a big boost in the past few years. The state is maintaining modest football academies and our club is in the process of starting a new residential academy that will offer academics besides quality football training.'

The advent of the ISL in 2014 brought about the formation of North-East United—a franchise representing the eight states of north-east India. Owned by Shillong Lajong, (which exited after year one) and Bollywood actor John Abraham, North-East United has caught the fancy of the football loving Assamese fans but is yet to replicate that success on the field.

Like Shillong Lajong in the past, Aizawl and NEROCA's recent successes could pave the way to success for clubs from northeast India, something that will only aid the development of Indian football in the long run. The influence and fertility of the northeastern states in Indian football's scheme of things can be gauged by the fact that the India U-17 team for the FIFA U-17 World Cup had ten out of the twenty-one players making the final squad coming from the north-east. The captain Amarjit Singh Kiyam also belonged to Manipur.

BENGALURU FC

Bengaluru FC came into being in 2013, entering the Indian top division—the I-League—directly winning the bid because of it being a corporate funded team. Jindal South West (JSW), one of India's largest steel conglomerates, was behind the birth of Bengaluru FC. On 20 June 2013, with Sunil Chhetri, Robin Singh, Thoi Singh, John Johnson among others, Bengaluru FC was born. This fast-tracked the growth of Indian football with a great professional set up.

BFC's Head Coach Ashley Westwood brought about a change in Indian football. Westwood, a former Manchester United academy player, had put BFC on track right from the outset. According to *MondoFootball*,[5] Westwood's principles were discipline, being professional and respect. 'Eighteen players (extended until twenty-one), led by former Middlesbrough [player] John Johnson and by the first team captain Sunil Chhetri, a reliable coaching staff, some pre-season friendlies (Bengaluru debuted against Indian national team), cast-iron diet, attention, investment in youth academy (their members won national phase MUPC, also called Nike Cup),' was how BFC started out. That approach has seen the club win four trophies in four years since its inception.

Two I-League titles and two Federation Cup wins since 2013 have firmly established BFC as the biggest club in Indian football. 'Simple ingredients but sufficient to win I-League title at their first attempt thanks to passionate and cheerful fans,' read the *MondoFootball* article, in one sentence capturing BFC's essence. All that would also stream through the rest of India, eventually preceding the birth of another big Indian football league—the Indian Super League.

The ISL started in 2014 and with it, Indian football got a much-needed shot in the arm with the glitz and the glamour. Bollywood celebrities were roped in as co-owners or ambassadors, and Indian football was never the same.

'I've said this many times before but will say it again, the ultimate dream would be to win the League with eleven Indian players on the field,' Bengaluru CEO and owner Parth Jindal stated in an interview speaking volumes of the ambition and drive and the tough path to realisation that Bengaluru FC were ready to take.

After reaching the 2016–17 AFC Cup Finals and losing to Air Force Club of Iraq, BFC have etched their name firmly in the Indian football history books. West Block Blues, their famed fan

---

[5] http://www.mondofutbol.com/en/bengaluru-football-club-young-but-already-great/

club, has brought in a culture of passionate chanting and in-ground support so far seen only in the western leagues. In 2017–18, Bengaluru FC jumped ships to now ply their trade in the Indian Super League. While continuing to represent India on the AFC stage, Bengaluru rubbed shoulders with the ISL teams and blazed through to the Finals of the Indian Super League after having topped the group stages.

Chennaiyin FC took the ISL trophy away from Bengaluru. Bengaluru also went to the AFC Cup 2017–18 Semi-Finals. A season without Bengaluru winning the trophy doesn't happen and they lifted the Super Cup 2018 trophy beating Mohun Bagan 4-2 in the Final. JSW Sports headed by Parth Jindal has massive investment in the entire landscape of Indian sports, owning franchise teams in Indian Premier League, Pro Kabaddi League as well as supporting a huge number of athletes in Olympic sports.

CHENNAIYIN FC AND CHENNAI CITY FC

Only two teams have shared the Indian Super League title in the first four seasons of its existence—Chennaiyin and ATK. A team owned by Vita Dani, Abhishek Bachchan and Mahendra Singh Dhoni—Chennaiyin has had some very impressive football on display with Brazilian playmaker Elano and Columbian striker Stiven Mendoza combining together to create havoc for opposition defences the first two seasons of the Indian Super League.

While Mendoza was the hero of the league in season two, Elano won the highest goalscorer award the first season. It was eventually injury to both the players that stopped the Chennaiyin juggernaut the first season of the ISL. While Elano returned to play a role later on in the league, he was not quite the same and Stiven's season was cut short after he made a breathtaking start to season one. Marco Materrazzi's last season in charge did not quite go according to plan and the team failed to make the Semis. Englishman John Gregory has been handed over the responsibility to spearhead the team to the title in his first season—against the more fancied teams.

A franchise entry into the I-League 2016–17, Chennai City FC has been playing in the local leagues for a long period of time. Started in 1946 as Nethaji Sports Club, Chennai City FC is now backed by Rohit Ramesh; it gained a direct entry in the 2016 edition of the I-League. After a slow start to the League which also saw huge challenges thrown in the way of the owners, Chennai City FC gained some foothold in the league and ultimately finished in the eighth place with four wins to their credit including a memorable one against East Bengal in Chennai. The club moved their base to Coimbatore to play the 2017–18 season from Tamil Nadu's second biggest city which has a decent history of football fervour. A much better showing saw the team end the season strongly with some players being picked by a host of ISL teams.

NORTH INDIA

While the likes of JCT have won national titles, the north of India is probably one of the most unrepresented areas as far as football in India is concerned. 2017–18 season was that of Minerva Punjab's as the team scripted yet another underdog story winning the I-League leading through the entire course of the league. If 2016–17 was North-East's I-League, 2017–18 was North India's.

Minerva won the I-League and Real Kashmir won the I-League 2.

DELHI DYNAMOS

Delhi Dynamos are the lone ISL side in the north of the country. The city of Delhi has generally seen apathy towards the sport in the recent past and has lacked organisational abilities to be able to capture the imagination of the young urban audience with great affinity to the sport. Dynamos have gone on and qualified twice for the semis of the Indian Super League inspired by their mercurial French attacking midfielders Florent Malouda and Brazilian Marcelinho in the third season.

Delhi Dynamos have been taken over by Dubai-based GMS Shipping and have partnered Aspire Group of Qatar to take the football fervour of the country's capital forward. 2017–18 didn't bring much joy to the this side as they finished a lowly seventh despite finishing very strongly in the league.

Hindustan FC, Delhi United and Sudeva Moonlight FC represented Delhi in the I-League 2 in the 2016–17 season, but lack of local support didn't see them present a challenge as strong as they are all capable of. Efforts are being made to turn the tide as far as Delhi football is concerned.

Former FIFA Development Officer (South and Central Asia) Shaji Prabhakaran is now the president of the Delhi Soccer Association. Shaji, a huge believer of Delhi's potential as a football city, says, 'Delhi football should be revived at all cost and we would like to contribute in the revival process by working closely with all the stakeholders of Delhi to make the National Capital Region one of the top football playing regions in India.'

MINERVA PUNJAB

Minerva Punjab FC has come onto the stage in the last few seasons as they finished a close second to Dempo SC in the I-League 2, 2015–16 season. Qualifying as a franchise team in the I-League in the 2016–17 season, Minerva put a very young team to the test, and while they did chest the tape at the end of the season slightly ahead of relegated Mumbai FC, season 17-18 was the turning point for the senior team of the club.

It has been on its way to becoming one of the best academy teams of the country, having provided several players to the national age group teams as well as winning almost every youth league that is on offer.

Minerva scripted the perfect I-League season winning the championship and staying ahead of all the other clubs through the season. Seeing the Mahilpur and Rurka Kalan programmes also producing some decent footballers for the country, Minerva need to ride the wave of youth in their next journey forward.

A young mercurial entrepreneur, Ranjit Bajaj, a former footballer himself, is leading the charge at Minerva Punjab and trust in youth talent seems to be the mantra for the club.

LONESTAR AND REAL KASHMIR

Another bright light in the North India football ecosystem was the performance of Real Kashmir last season as the Srinagar team won the I-League 2 led by former Glasgow Rangers great Dave Robertson.

Lonestar Kashmir also did well in the second division and would need more encouragement to continue competing with Delhi sides such as Hindustan FC, Delhi United and Sudeva Moonlight in the second division. There is no doubt that the northern part of India needs far more investment in football than is happening right now.

THE CHANGE OF LEAGUES LEADING TO CHANGE IN CLUBS

With time, ISL clubs have grown their fan bases and subsequently given the league a profile to rub shoulders with the world. India has never had a world-class nationwide football league. The National Football League's inception by the AIFF in 1996 ushered in a new chapter in Indian football but that proved only to be a delusion of grandeur. The AIFF, with Philips as the sponsor, started a semi-professional national league—the first of its kind in Indian football history. However, ten years later, to retool Indian football, the I-League was established as the top division. While the NFL saw the dominance of Mohun Bagan and East Bengal, the final days of the old top flight suggested a change of guard from Kolkata to Goa.

Goan clubs emerged as serious contenders for the NFL title and Dempo won two of the last three NFL seasons. Dempo, from

Goa, has since gone on to dominate the I-League in its early years. The club has won the I-League title thrice. In fact, three Goan clubs—Dempo, Salgaocar and Churchill Brothers—swept the first six I-League titles until the new wave called Bengaluru FC came about. The glorious Goan chapter was about to close—the new boys from Bengaluru were the talk of the town.

Bengaluru FC, as mentioned earlier, has been immensely successful on and off the pitch. The club has set an example for Indian football with its progression to the ISL. The ISL, through its western model of professional sports, has adopted a franchise-based system and its teams are run more professionally than before. The success of the league is now more important than ever owing to it getting recognition[6] from FIFA and the AFC.

What the ISL started was the model Bengaluru FC built upon. These two joining hands will only serve to benefit Indian football in the longer run. For the shorter run, the FIFA U-17 World Cup provided the launch pad for India to enter the football elite, which with the help of the ISL and clubs like BFC and the other ISL franchises, will only strengthen with the passage of time.

Just like Indian football legend PK Banerjee noted before the world cup,[7] 'The time has come for the boys [the India U-17 players] to give their life for the World Cup. We never had such an opportunity in our days. Take India to the next level…'

---

[6] http://www.goal.com/en-in/news/indian-football-isl-gets-recognition-from-afc-and-fifa/gdvxrob0spvu1tei948rtj295

[7] http://timesofindia.indiatimes.com/sports/football/under-17-world-cup/news/use-u-17-world-cup-to-secure-indias-future-as-football-nation-pk-banerjee/articleshow/60477036.cms

CHAPTER 5
INDIAN LEAGUES AND TOURNAMENTS

Leagues—both senior leagues and age group leagues—give the players an opportunity to regularly test themselves, ascertain their progress and have coaches to identify and guide the way forward. Organisation has been India's biggest failing in its quest for relevance in the competitive football scenario in the world. Ability to organise and structure leagues, give football the pan-India structure, marry ability, marketing and commercialisation with the technical aspect of the sport, organisation of grassroots and youth development and bridging this gap from the bottom of the pyramid to the top of the pyramid (elite leagues).

It is not that there was no understanding of how the leagues are operated. However, unlike the European countries where close proximity of clubs to one another geographically makes it easier for them to travel and play each other, it was a tough task to formulate a central league where teams from all across India would play.

So various different leagues operated in local clusters, with Calcutta Football League as the prime example. This does not mean that the powers at the helm did not want to see teams from different parts of the country compete against each other. They definitely did.

The tournament format made the movement to one part of the country, staying at one place, playing games against teams from other parts of the country and then moving back, possible. A firm tournament culture established itself in India. It brought regularity and quorum to clubs.

The result is that India saw some of the oldest and most historic tournaments taking shape over the past century since football has existed in this country.

TOURNAMENTS

India is the home of the biggest and oldest football tournaments in the world. The IFA Shield, Durand Cup, Rovers Cup, Federation Cup, Santosh Trophy, Indian Super Cup and Subroto Cup are, or have been, some of the major competitive tournaments played in India.

The concept and importance of the leagues, especially of a pan-Indian league, was fairly alien to early day teams and hence these teams primarily competed with each other in marquee tournaments. There was an odd league like the Calcutta Football League but primarily the competition in the sport was confined to tournaments. Over the years, these competitions have lost some of their star value and some have gone into oblivion.

The 2016 edition of India's oldest and world's third most seasoned competition Durand Cup played between Manipur's NEROCA and Defence Force's very own Army XI saw an energising finale, in spite of missing out on great or established teams.

It showed how small teams could have a tremendous impact if given a consistent open door. Notwithstanding few I-League clubs like Dempo, DSK Shivajians, Aizawl FC partaking in the competitions, it was two first timers that achieved the grand finale, which was immensely welcomed by the crowd who turned out in the stadiums.

Some of India's top or the 'once' top tournaments are discussed further.

DURAND CUP

The Durand Cup was named after its founder Sir Mortimer Durand, Foreign Secretary in-charge of India from 1884–94. It is one of the oldest tournaments and was first presented as a prize to encourage the sporting competition in India.

In the 128th Durand Football Tournament, Army Green came out victorious against a very spirited NEROCA FC (Manipur)

6-5 in a penalty shootout. It was a real moment of victory when NEROCA's experienced defender Govin Singh hit the post with his attempt and Army substitute Bikram Adhikari calmly stepped up and placed the ball to the left of goalkeeper Lalit Thapa. Proud and delighted jawans gathered at the Ambedkar Stadium stood up to cheer for them.

The venue of the tournament was changed in 1940 from Dagshai to New Delhi and it is now held at the Ambedkar Stadium in the city.

The winning team is presented with three trophies—The President's Cup (first presented by Dr Rajendra Prasad, the first President of India), the Durand Cup (the original challenge prize, which is a rolling trophy), and the Shimla Trophy (first presented by citizens of Shimla in 1904 and, since 1965, a rolling trophy).

India's armed forces deserve credit for keeping the Durand Cup tradition alive over the decades. Since 2006, Osians, the art house, have been responsible for the running and management of the Durand Cup.

IFA SHIELD

The IFA Shield came into existence in 1893. The IFA Shield Tournament is one of India's oldest football tournaments and the fourth oldest Cup in the world.

During the initial years, British army teams always won the IFA Shield. However, that changed in 1911, when Mohun Bagan Athletic Club became the first Indian team to win the IFA Shield by defeating East Yorkshire Regiment 2-1. Being the pre-independence era, that became a historic moment for Indian football, as the natives beat the Englishmen at their own game. The team of 1911 is still remembered as the immortal eleven and will remain so forever. Mohun Bagan became synonymous with 'Vande Mataram'.

The other big club from Kolkata, East Bengal FC, has won the IFA Shield twenty-nine times, while their arch rivals—Mohun Bagan—have won it twenty-two times. The involvement of foreign teams has been one of the USPs of IFA Shield.

East Bengal's win over Pas club of Tehran was the first victory of an Indian club over a foreign club since 1947. Since 2015, the IFA decided to design the tournament as an Under-19 youth football tournament.

ROVERS CUP

The Rovers Cup was a football tournament held in India. British football enthusiasts at Bombay started it in 1891. Worcester Regiment was the winner in the inaugural year. The Western India Football Association (WIFA) is making efforts to revive the tournament. At present, former footballers want the revival of the prestigious Rovers Cup in Mumbai.

The tournament boasted of some big names, and ever since it was stopped, local fans have been deprived of some top-level football. Given the popularity of clubs like Mohun Bagan in Mumbai, the spectator turnout for the games was quite high. The Rovers Cup worked essentially like the IPL, where youngsters could watch the top players live, taking inspiration from them. However, considering the AIFF's plans to increase the duration of the Indian Super League (ISL) and I-League, it will be difficult to find a window in the annual calendar for this tournament.

The last time Rovers Cup was held was in the 2000–01 season, when Mohun Bagan beat Churchill Brothers Sports Club from Goa 2-0 in the Final. It shut down due to a legal case over availability of the Cooperage—the venue for the tournament. The legal issues have now been resolved. Initially, British regimental teams dominated this tournament.

Mohun Bagan became the first Indian club to reach the final in 1923. Bangalore Muslims was the first Indian team to win the tournament in 1937. They were the most successful team in the history of Rovers Cup, winning the coveted crown a grand fourteen times, besides securing the runners-up trophy on another ten occasions. East Bengal is the second most successful team in Rovers Cup with ten Champions and four runners-up crowns.

SUBROTO CUP

Named after the Indian Air Force Air Marshal Subroto Mukerjee, Subroto Cup Football Tournament is one of the famous inter-school football tournaments in India. The tournament was started in 1960, with the participation of about fifty school teams with even schools from Nepal and Afghanistan participating over the years. Since 1998, the tournament is played in two age groups, sub-Junior (U14) and Junior (U-17). Madhyamgram High School, West Bengal, is famous for winning this tournament (U-17) seven times including getting a hat-trick in the matches held from 1981–83.

Subroto Cup is conducted by the Indian Air Force, with support from India's Ministry of Youth Affairs and Sports. Preliminary inter-school tournaments are held in every state of India and the school teams winning the state inter-school championships are then invited to participate in the main Subroto Mukerjee Cup Tournament at Delhi.

The tournament also hosts many well-known football legends as chief guests like Brazilian legend and football's elder statesman Pele who graced the final of the 56th edition of the Subroto Cup with his presence.

SANTOSH TROPHY

Santosh Trophy is an annual Indian football tournament contested between states and government institutions. The first winners were Bengal, who are also leading the all-time winners list with thirty-one titles to date. Before the start of the first national club league—the National Football League—in 1996, the Santosh Trophy was considered the top domestic championship in India. Many players who have represented India internationally played and gained fame playing in the Santosh Trophy. The tournament is held every year with thirty-one teams that are divided into groups and who must qualify for the tournament through the preliminary round. The 2016–17 champions were West Bengal, who won their 32nd title followed by Kerala in the 2017–18 season.

The tournament was started in 1941 and is named after the President of the Indian Football Association (West Bengal's Football Association) at the time—Sir Manmatha Nath Roy Chowdhary of Santosh. The IFA were the ones who donated the Santosh Trophy. An ex-IFA President, SK Gupta, also donated the runners-up trophy. The trophy is known as the Kamla Gupta Trophy. The Karnataka State Football Association (then the Mysore Football Association) donated the third-place trophy, the Sampangi Cup.

INDIAN SUPER CUP

Much like the Community Shield in England, the Indian Super Cup is a one-off annual Indian Club Association Football match, contested between the I-League champions and the Fed Cup winners. If the winner in the I-League as well as Federation Cup is the same, then the league runners-up become the second team. The winners of the game receive the shield as a trophy for the year, while players receive individual winner's medals.

Starting out in 1997, the tournament has been held eleven times. It was cancelled in 2000–02 and then restarted in 2011. East Bengal FC has won it three times, while Dempo, Salgaocar and Mohun Bagan each won it twice.

A revamped version of the Super Cup was introduced in 2018 which saw a qualifier between 7-10 ranked teams taking on 1-6 ranked teams of the I-League and ISL.

Bengaluru FC emerged winners of the trophy beating East Bengal in the Finals.

FEDERATION CUP

Starting in 1977, the Federation Cup is a once-a-year knockout style club football tournament in India. The winner of this tournament gets a chance to compete at Continental level in AFC Cup.

The current holders of the Federation Cup are Bengaluru FC who beat Mohun Bagan AC 2-0 in the 2017 Final held in Cuttack, Odisha. In April 2015, All India Football Federation announced that Federation Cup would be put 'on hold' for 'two-three years' to avoid scheduling conflict with Indian Super League and I-League.

After Asian Football Confederation mandated that a club must play eighteen matches in the season, AIFF decided to revive the tournament. Fed Cup, as the tournament is more popularly known, has given the Indian football fans many interesting matches, filled with passion, drama, elation and sadness.

The list of five of the most intriguing Fed Cup Finals held in recent history:

Mohun Bagan 2-1 East Bengal, 1998

The rivalry between Mohun Bagan and East Bengal has been well documented over the years. No other derby in the world can match up to the Kolkata Derby. Over a hundred thousand people flocked to the stadium to see who would win.

On this fateful day, legendary Indian midfielder IM Vijayan stole the show, and the cup, from the Red and Gold, as he scored the winning goal. This was Mohun Bagan's tenth Fed Cup title.

Dempo SC 2-0 Mohun Bagan, 2004

Dempo's Brazilian striker Cristiano Jr was in top form, and he completely routed the Mohun Bagan defence, scoring both the goals in a 2-0 win over the Kolkata giants.

Instead of being remembered for his heroics, Cristiano Junior will be remembered more for the tragedy that struck him as he stroked the ball past Bagan keeper Subrata Pal. The young keeper, while trying to put off the striker, seemed to have punched Cristiano on the face. The Brazilian immediately went down, visibly uncomfortable. He was later taken to the hospital, where he was announced dead.

Cristiano Junior's death was one of the greatest tragedies the Fed Cup had ever seen.

East Bengal 3-0 Shillong Lajong FC, 2009-10

East Bengal faced Shillong Lajong in the Final. Both the teams played out a drab 0-0 draw in normal and extra time, and it was down to the penalties to decide the winner.

East Bengal keeper Abhra Mondal showed his heroics once again, as he saved four penalties to give his team a 3-0 victory in the shootout. Ironically, it was the man from the North-East—Sanju Pradhan—who scored the winning penalty for the Red and Gold brigade.

East Bengal 1-0 Mohun Bagan, 2010

The final, held in Cuttack, saw no reduction in the support for either of the teams, with the venue situated relatively close to Kolkata. That, however, did not stop Reisangmei Vashum from scoring a fifty-third minute winner, as the Red and Gold brigade ran away with a 1-0 win and their seventh Fed Cup title.

East Bengal 3-2 Dempo SC, 2012

In one of the finest finals of Federation Cup history, East Bengal faced Dempo. In Siliguri, West Bengal, the Red and Gold brigade had full support of the local crowd. They went in as favourites to lift the trophy for the eighth time.

Clinical as ever, Dempo took the lead twice—first in normal time and then in the extra time. However, East Bengal were also up to the task, equalising on both occasions to keep their chances alive. At the end of it, it was East Bengal's Nigerian striker Edeh Chidi who scored a hundred and ninth minute winner to clinch the prestigious cup for his side in extra time.

THE LEAGUES

Realising that mere tournaments would not help in furthering the popularity of football amongst Indian audiences, and to professionalise a sport that was moving at breathtaking speed across the world—the AIFF decide to launch the first pan India Football League in the country. While it was indeed an opportunity for any team across the country to participate, the NFL essentially wanted a true representative for every nook and corner of India.

NFL AND I-LEAGUE

In 1996, the first domestic league known as the National Football League was started in India. The league was started in an effort to introduce professionalism in Indian football. Despite the ambition, that has never been achieved. During the National Football League days, the league suffered from poor infrastructure and unprofessionalism from its clubs.

After the FC Kochin fiasco where the club encountered loss of 2.5 crores and the decade of decline with the National Football League, the All India Football Federation decided it was time for a change and the rebranding of the top-tier in India, which resulted in the making of I-League.

As a new rule, all the clubs could sign four foreigners—three non-Asian ones and one Asian, and the first season matches would be broadcast on *Zee Sports*.

I-LEAGUE SEASON CHAMPIONS

2007–08	Dempo
2008–09	Churchill Brothers
2009–10	Dempo
2010–11	Salgaocar
2011–12	Dempo
2012–13	Churchill Brothers
2013–14	Bengaluru FC
2014–15	Mohun Bagan
2015–16	Bengaluru FC
2016–17	Aizawl
2017–18	Minerva Punjab FC

The first ever I-League match took place on 24 November 2007 between Dempo and Salgaocar. The match which took place at the Fatorda Stadium in Margao, ended 3-0 in favour of Dempo, with Chidi Edeh scoring the first ever goal in league history in the third minute. After eighteen rounds, Dempo came out as the first ever champions in the I-League. Viva Kerala and Salgaocar, however, ended up as the first two teams to ever be relegated from the I-League.

The next season, the I-League was expanded from ten to twelve teams. Mumbai, Chirag United, Mohammedan and Vasco were all promoted from the I-League Second Division to make the expansion possible. This, however, brought up early concerns over how 'national' the I-League was. The 2008–09 season saw eleven of the twelve teams coming from three different cities. The previous season saw all ten teams coming from four different cities.

Bhaichung Bhutia, then captain of the Indian National Team said, 'Efforts should be made to see that more clubs representing different states are present in the top league of the country.'

Regardless of the early criticism, I-League gained a more pan India foothold after 2009–10 season as then the league played in seven different cities/states—Goa, Kerala, Kolkata, Mumbai, Pune, Punjab and Shillong.

Dempo FC won the league for the second time. Gradually, the league managed to improve its product on the field and awareness also increased during this period. While the league continued to be fairly salient in strong footballing cities such as Kolkata and Goa, it was seeing huge traction in towns like Shillong where people thronged to the stadium to witness their local team, comprising of all north-easterners, play against the best football teams in the country.

The Indian team at this point in time was doing fairly well. It had qualified for the 2011 AFC Asian Cup. Despite being knocked-out in the group stage after losing all the three of their games, India came back home more popular than ever. Football, along with the footballers had gained a fair bit of importance across the country, especially in the football playing centres.

The league was then given a major boost from its main derby, the Kolkata derby, between East Bengal and Mohun Bagan. On 20 November 2011, ninety thousand people watched at the Salt Lake Stadium when Mohun Bagan defeated East Bengal 1-0. The league also saw expansion to others areas with the promotion of United Sikkim from the Second Division. However, their reign was short-lived as they were almost instantly relegated. The success of Shillong Lajong also saw a wave of north-east teams upping the ante and looking to qualify for the I-League.

In the last seven editions of the I-League, where the top team goes on to qualify for the I-League, six winners were from the north-east, barring the 2015-16 season, in which Dempo won. Shillong Lajong won the Division Two in 2011, followed by United Sikkim, Rangdajied, Royal Wahigdoh, Aizawl and most recently NEROCA and Real Kashmir. With five teams in the 2016-17 from the eastern part of the country, this could have been the most relevant league to the East of India, with at least six north-east derbies and many eastern derbies. It could have provided the spark needed by the league.

Meanwhile, while the league continued to grow, so did the demand for players. During this period, foreign clubs, mainly in Europe, wanted plenty of Indian players on trial. After his return from MLS, Sunil Chhetri and international teammate Jeje Lalpekhlua moved in for a trial with Scottish side Rangers. Subrata Pal had trials at RB Leipzig before finally signing for Danish club Vestsjælland in 2014. In addition, Gurpreet Singh Sandhu underwent trials at the Premier League side Wigan Athletic and finally signed for Stabæk Fotball, Norway in 2014.

At the same time, as demand of Indian players increased abroad, the demand for higher quality foreigners in the I-League also increased. Former A-League player of the year and Costa Rican international Carlos Hernández from the Melbourne Victory signed with Prayag United before the 2012–13 season. Lebanese international Bilal Najjarine also signed with Churchill Brothers in 2012.

Since the league began in 2007 the rules of the league have changed quite a bit. Last edition of the I-League saw participation from ten teams. Each club played each other twice during the season, once at home and the other away from home. The team that would win a match received three points while both the teams gained one point each if there was a draw. The losing team was not awarded any point. At the end of the season, the team with the most points would win the league. In case of a tie the head to head record had to be looked upon. Further, in the case of a tie, the goal difference was also looked at of the tied teams.

The league has also seen an uncertain future even though the AIFF had repeatedly stated that it is the top league of the country. High profile clubs such as Mahindra United, JCT, United SC, Pune FC, Sporting Club De Goa, Dempo SC, Salgaocar, Royal Wahindoh, Rangdajied have all either shut down operations or moved out of the league citing lack of clarity in the roadmap for Indian football.

A merger or selective inclusion has been mooted by the Asian Football Confederation between the Indian Super League and I-League which promises to push the development of Indian football.

SIX MOST MEMORABLE I-LEAGUE CAMPAIGNS

2010–11: Salgaocar won the I-League as well as the Federation Cup, while four bottom-placed teams finished at twenty-four points each

It was a season where Goa's Salgaocar FC led by Moroccan Coach Karim Bencherifa clinched the League. The highlight was that four teams at the bottom of the table finished with 24 points each. In the lead-up to the final day of the season, equations had become fairly complex with the three teams competing to avoid joining relegation.

ONGC were already clear about their future, which was in the second division. HAL, Bengaluru who were at the bottom of the table could save relegation if they beat a strong Dempo side. JCT who were safe from relegation going into the last match-day could be dragged in to being relegated if HAL beat Dempo. Air India also finished the season with 24 points with the worst goal difference of -32. However, in the I-League, 'head to head' is considered as the differentiation if teams finish on the same points.

As luck would have it, HAL beat Dempo and JCT, the first team to win the NFL. Ranti Martins and Odafa Okolie, two of I-League's most prolific scorers, kept their competition on scoring twenty-eight and twenty-five goals respectively. Salgaocar, buoyed by eighteen and fifteen goal haul of Ryuji Sueoka and Yusif Yakubu proved too strong for the rest of the field, winning the I-League with fifty-six points. Salgaocar also grabbed eleven clean sheets and failed to score in only three games through the season. Young players such as Gilbert Oliveira and Francis Fernandes showcased their ability guided by experienced Luciano Sabrosa at the back.

2009–10: Dempo powered its way to the title

The Goan powerhouse were a tough unit to face. They won the 2009–10 season bagging fifty-four points. Their closest rivals Churchill Brothers were eleven points adrift at forty-three with Pune FC at forty-two. Dempo became the most successful football club in India with this win, having won the top Division in India for a record fourth time.

The season saw the I-League adopt AFC's new 3+1 foreigners rule where teams were to pick one Asian amongst their contingent of four foreigners. Coach Armando Colaco marshalled his troops brilliantly with Ranti Martins 'amongst the goals'. Dempo ended the season with a net goal difference of twenty-three having scored fifty-four goals and conceded thirty-one goals.

Interestingly, few teams in the league conceded fewer goals than Dempo with Pune conceding twenty-three, Mahindra United and JCT twenty-nine goals; the highlight was Mumbai FC which coached by Khalid Jamil conceded only twenty-six goals. It was Khalid's first season as a senior team coach and while his team could manage only twenty-four goals—less than half of Dempo's—his goals conceded tally was better than the champions. This defensive solidity has become the highlight of his career so far.

2014–15: Bagan took home Kolkata's first I-League title

Bengaluru FC had announced their entry as India's top new entrants while Kolkata was waiting for its first ever I-League title. Since the NFL was rechristened, the I-League's first six winners were all Goan clubs. Bengaluru had won the title in its first ever season. Bagan seemed to be on a mission with Sanjoy Sen taking over the reins of the club in December 2014.

The curtailed I-League season which was to start in January saw Bagan on the front foot right from the beginning having compiled a very strong squad of players. Haitian Sony Norde, Japanese Katsumi Yusa, Bello Rasaq, Pierre Boya, Jeje Lalpekhlua, Balwant Singh, Dhanachandra Singh, Sehnaj Singh, Debjit

Majumder all turned out in the maroon and green as they went into the last round of the league needing a draw away from home against arch-rivals and second placed Bengaluru FC.

A 41st minute header by English defender John Johnson off a Eugeneson Lyngdoh corner saw Bagan's hopes of landing the coveted trophy hang in the balance early on. All of Bagan's efforts, witnessed by a strong contingent of their fans didn't result in a goal till the 86th minute when Bello Rasaq rose high to head a Sony Norde corner into the net. A famous draw handed Bagan the national title after a long wait.

2013–14: Bengaluru FC form a club, enter the I-League and win it!

The first ever franchise team in the I-League Bengaluru FC entered the competition in 2013–14. Owned by JSW, the garden city team appointed former Manchester United youth player Ashley Westwood as their Head Coach; former Shillong Lajong Head Coach Pradhyum Reddy was brought in as his assistant and the club went about getting ready for their first season in the biggest league of football in India. Barring Sunil Chhetri and Robin Singh, both of whom were well known I-League stars at that time, almost all the other players who came in were not top stars at that point of time in India.

Ashely Westwood recruited John Johnson and Curtis Osana to join Johny Meyongar and Sean Rooney as the club's four foreigners. Indian players like Rino Anto, Thoi Singh, Pawan Kumar, Keegan Pereira, Siam Hanghal, Beikhokhei Beingaichho weren't the established names then. Bengaluru almost revolutionised the way everything related to football was run in India with great focus on player management—their diet, recovery, stay, travel and overall well-being, coupled with great match-day organisation, media outreach, social media and fan activities.

Sunil Chhetri moved to a new position on the left as he, along with Sean Rooney, shared twenty-five goals amongst them with a very strong defensive unit conceding very few goals through the season. Bengaluru scored forty-two goals in the season as they raked forty-seven points from twenty-four games beating East Bengal by four points at the top of the table.

Before Bengaluru, for six continuous seasons in the I-League, Goan teams had ruled the roost. Bengaluru had started a revolution of sorts and could be seen as a turning point for football in India with their modern approach. They went on and won the 2015–16 I-League title in addition to winning the Federation Cup twice over the next three seasons before moving on to play in the Indian Super League from season 2017–18.

2017–18: Minerva Punjab, bulldozing its way to the title

Minerva entered the I-League in 2016–17. Despite finishing the second division at second place and Dempo not taking up the climb up to the I-League, Minerva was only brought in as a franchise corporate team. Finishing right ahead of the relegated Mumbai FC in the second season, Minerva absolutely pulverised the opposition and bulldozed its way through to the title in 2017–18. Taking unfancied young players, Indian and foreign, Minerva put together a cohesive hard working unit that played compact football that broke through with pace and decisiveness.

Bhutanese import Chencho Gyeltshen was almost unstoppable through the league and ended up becoming the player of the season. William Opuku, Kaisam Aidara, Rakhsit Dagar, Abhishek Ambekar, Bali Gagandeep were amongst the many players that were picked up by bigger fancied clubs after the season. Minerva won eleven games, two more than NEROCA, with Chencho scoring seven goals, Opoku five and Balli Gagandeep three goals.

2016–17: Aizawl FC: Miracle of Mizoram

Aizawl FC qualified for the 2015–16 season of the I-League becoming the first team from Mizoram to do so. However, the first season didn't go well for the side as they finished eighth in a nine-team league after Pune FC, Bharat FC and Royal Wahingdoh had pulled out of the I-League before the beginning of the season.

While DSK Shivajians finished last on the table they were granted immunity by virtue of them being a franchise team. Beginning of 2016–17 season saw three Goan teams—Sporting Club de Goa, Salgaocar SC and Dempo SC who were the I-League 2 Champions pull out of the I-League. Aizawl were instated in the league with two new franchise teams Minerva Punjab FC and Chennai City FC joining the league.

Former Mumbai FC Coach Khalid Jamil was appointed Aizawl's coach and he brought in Albino Gomes and his former Mumbai boys Ashutosh Mehta and Jayesh Rane along with him, in addition to a strong Mizo squad which included upcoming players such as Brandon Vanlalremdika, Laldanmawia Ralte, Lalruatthara, Lalramchullova and Zohmingliana Ralte.

Former Sporting Club De Goa midfielder, Mahmoud Al Amnah, joined the squad along with Alfred Jaryan, Obumneme Kingsley and Bayi Kamo as the squad's four foreigners. Aizawl garnered ten points from the opening four games of the season as they drew East Bengal away from home before adding wins against Minerva, Lajong and Mumbai.

One of their three defeats came against new entrants Chennai City FC. Mohun Bagan and Bengaluru were the only other sides to have beaten Aizawl in the season as they went on an unbeaten seven game run winning five of those games. As the season took shape and Aizawl were still leading the table, they garnered a lot of attention across India.

Press conferences which had become mundane at a lot of I-League venues, started bustling with reporters wherever the team Aizawl went. 'Will they, wont they' was a question which was being asked everywhere. Leicester had done it in the Premier League. Would a club from Mizoram be able to do the unthinkable?

While it may have come as a shock to everyone, Mizoram has been a powerhouse in the making for quite some time. Football is a religion in the north-east state and there is no village in the state which doesn't have a football club. They burst into national prominence having won the Santosh Trophy (State Championship) in 2014.

What Aizawl was about to achieve seemed improbable. For a state that has produced quality football players for various clubs in the country, a fairy tale was in the making. Aizawl FC needed a draw going into the last game of the season with Shillong Lajong. Mohun Bagan were playing Chennai City at home and only an Aizawl FC loss combined with their win could have given them the Championship. An early Dipanda Dicka goal gave Bagan some hope despite them going behind to Chennai. Aizawl however did get the goal and the point they went to Shillong for. Aizawl were the Champions of India and there might not be another story like Aizawl FC any time soon.

I-LEAGUE STATS AT A QUICK GLANCE

Dempo SC have won the national title a maximum of 5 times (NFL-2, I-League-3), Mohun Bagan 4 times (NFL-3, I-League-1), East Bengal 3 times (NFL-3), Salgaocar Club 2 (NFL-1, I-League-1), Churchill Brothers 2 (I-League-2), Bengaluru FC 2 (I-League-2), JCT 1 (NFL-1), Mahindra United 1 (NFL-1), Minerva 1 (I-League-1) and Aizawl 1 (I-Leauge-1). No team has won the title three years in a row. East Bengal (2002–03, 2003–04) and Dempo Club (2006–07, 2007–08) have won the title two years in a row. East Bengal has recorded the maximum of 194 wins in NFL/I-League (till end of 2017 18 season).

East Bengal hold the record of being unbeaten in twenty-two consecutive matches from January, 2002–April, 2003 of NFL. Mohun Bagan recorded the maximum of ten consecutive wins in 2008–09 I-League. Churchill Brothers have scored the maximum of 623 goals in NFL and I-League.

Leading Scorers

1. Ranti Martins   185 goals
2. Odafa Okolie   165 goals
3. Yusif Yakubu   146 goals
4. Chidi Edeh   103 goals
5. Jose Barreto   101 goals
6. Bhaichung Bhutia   89 goals
7. Sunil Chhetri   79 goals

Highest Scorer in One Edition

Ranti Martins (Dempo) scored 32 goals in 2011–12 edition of the I-League.

Maximum Goals by an Individual in One Match

Ranti Martins (Dempo) scored seven goals vs Air India on 30 May 2011, Margao.

Dempo Club have scored the maximum of 63 goals in one edition in 2010–11.

Dempo recorded the highest margin of victory when they defeated Air India 14-0 on 30 May 2011, Margao. This match also recorded the maximum number of goals in one match.

Dempo won the League with maximum of fifty-seven points in 2011–12.

AFC QUALIFICATION

Clubs from the I-League primarily participated internationally in the AFC Cup. Some I-League clubs have had the chance to qualify for the AFC Champions League. From 2007–11 the champions of the previous season of the I-League were allowed to play in a qualifier for the AFC Champions League. Then from 2011–13, no

I-League club played in a qualifier until Pune in 2014 after the club cleared the AFC Licensing Criteria.

However, to this day, no I-League has qualified for the AFC Champions League. From 2017–18 season, Champion of I-League, (Minerva in this case) will get a shot at AFC Champions League qualifier whereas AFC Cup spot will go to Indian Super League winners Chennaiyin.

CHAPTER 6
INDIAN SUPER LEAGUE

Along the way the sport became commercially viable and financially attractive as a technically robust structure was added to the sport of football. This sums up the objectives that Reliance-IMG combination could have charted out in the simplest fashion before launching the biggest effort for a league that India had seen so far.

The National Football League ultimately provided a pan India football league for the country in 1996. While it did tick all the boxes related to the presence and operation of a league in the country, it did nothing more than that. The organisation and professionalism that the modern day sport required probably was a fair distance away. Technically it provided the teams and players a platform to perform, but otherwise there was barely anything else that could attract the fans and crowds back to football in an atmosphere which was lucrative.

It still relied upon an East Bengal-Mohun Bagan-Mohammedan Sporting rivalry to draw crowds, something which had been happening in the Calcutta Football League for large parts of the century. The national footprint NFL had barely added any extras to the football scenario. Technical improvement and professionalism did improve with the rebranding exercise of the NFL through the I-League as more and more teams began running as private enterprises, complying to AFC licensing guidelines and employing professionals to run the sport in all its aspect.

Yet, the game lacked two key ingredients that modern day football has close association with—fan entrenchment and high quality match-day organisation. The Indian Super League was started with the aim of bridging this lacunae in Indian football.

The genesis of the Indian Super League began with Reliance Industries and International Management Group acquiring the rights to Indian football in 2010. In December 2010, it was announced that AIFF had signed a fifteen-year, 700 crore deal with Reliance-IMG joint venture. The deal gave IMG–Reliance exclusive commercial rights to sponsorship, advertising, broadcasting, merchandising, video, franchising and the right to create a new football league.

Plans for a revamped league were announced as Reliance-IMG joined with AIFF and started meeting key stakeholders across India discussing the possibility of revamping the I-League. This move was met with stiff opposition from existing stakeholders in Indian football, primarily because in certain ways it undermined their importance in the football ecology of India. Finally, at the end of 2013, it was announced that the proposed Indian Super League would incubate eight new teams, and by April 2014 bids were presented and Indian Football League calendar was broken into two phases with the Indian Super League taking place from October to December and the I-League from January onwards.

BACKGROUND

The Indian Super League (ISL) currently shares the top spot in the Indian football league system with the I-League. The league originally began with eight new incubated teams in 2014 (or franchises as they were called), but now comprises ten teams and runs for five months from November to March starting with the 2017–18 season.

The 2018–19 season will be a seven-month league format. The 2017–18 season had to be curtailed due to the FIFA U-17 World Cup that took place in India in October 2017. *Star Sports* was brought on board as a partner in the inaugural season of the Indian Super League to form Football Sports Development Private Limited (FSDL) with each one of Reliance, International Management Group and *Star Sports* as one third partners in the private limited company. The rights to the Indian Super League are now owned by this company.

During the first three seasons of the Indian Super League, it operated without official recognition from the Asian Football Confederation, the governing body for the sport in Asia. It was accorded the status of a tournament. However, before the 2017–18 season, the league earned recognition from the AFC, expanded to ten teams and extended its schedule to five months with the winners of the Indian Super League earning themselves a continental cup play-off spot in the AFC Cup.

At that time inception bids were invited from individuals, companies, clubs and consortiums where bidders would need to comply with not only financial requirements but they would also need to promote grassroots development plans for football within their club's area of operation. In early April 2014, the winning bidders were announced. The selected cities or states were Bengaluru, Delhi, Goa, Guwahati, Kochi, Kolkata, Mumbai, and Pune.

Indian cricket icon Sachin Tendulkar, along with PVP Ventures won the bid for the Kochi franchise. Another former Indian legend Sourav Ganguly teamed up with noted businessmen Sanjiv Goenka, Harshvardhan Neotia, Utsav Parekh and brought in La Liga giants Atlético Madrid to win the bid for the Kolkata franchise competing against a strong bidder in Shah Rukh Khan and his Kolkata Knight-Riders' franchise. Ranbir Kapoor teamed up with Bimal Parekh to stake claim to the Mumbai franchise. The rights to Bengaluru franchise were awarded to Sun group and Delhi was won by Den Networks. Goa was won by a consortium of Videocon Industries, Dattaraj Salgaocar, and I-League side Dempo represented by owner Srinivas Dempo. Later, current Indian Cricket Captain Virat Kohli was brought on board to complete the Goa Team. Shillong Lajong were the second I-League team to feature in the Indian Super League after winning the bid to Guwahati with another Indian film actor John Abraham. Pune went to Wadhawan group who brought in Italian side Fiorentina as partners.

There were a few misses as Sun Groups' effort for a partnership with Bengaluru FC failed early on, and added to certain other factors led to the group's early exit from the league. That saw the team shifting base from Bengaluru to Chennai as Vita Dani became the first woman majority owner of an ISL franchise teaming up with Abhishek Bachchan and the then captain of the Indian Cricket Team Mahendra Singh Dhoni. This set the stage for the first ever Indian Super League, which was held in India in October 2014.

The first team to be launched officially was the Kolkata franchise as Atlético de Kolkata on 7 May 2014. On 7 July 2014, the team announced the first Head Coach in league history—Antonio López Habas. The next day, Kolkata also announced the first official marquee signing in the Indian Super League, UEFA Champions League winner Luis García.

Eventually, eight teams were revealed as:

- Atlético de Kolkata
- Delhi Dynamos
- FC Goa
- Kerala Blasters
- Mumbai City
- North East United (Guwahati)
- Pune City
- Chennaiyin FC

Each one of the teams was mandated to have a marquee player and a marquee Coach to increase the profile of the league. Some very interesting names came down to India to play the inaugural edition of the Indian Super League—Luis García (Kolkata), Elano (Chennai), Alessandro Del Piero (Delhi), Robert Pirès (Goa), David James (Kerala), Fredrik Ljungberg (Mumbai), Joan Capdevila (Guwahati), and David Trezeguet (Pune) all lined up for their respective teams in Season 1. The ISL employed the 6+5 rule for the first three seasons, which meant that six foreigners would line up with five Indian players in the starting XI of the game. From 2017 onwards, this was changed to a compulsory six Indian players required on the pitch at any point in time.

Player draft and auction have been used in various formats in the Indian Super League right from inception up until date with normal open transfer market expected to be reinstated from 2018–19 season onwards. The ISL is a 'closed league', which means that unlike most other leagues across the world the participants of the league are not relegated at the end of the season for finishing at the lower positions in the league nor are teams brought up from lower leagues after having finished top.

The inaugural season began on 12 October 2014 at the Salt Lake Stadium when Atlético de Kolkata defeated Mumbai City, 3-0, with Fikru Teferra getting the first ever goal in the Indian Super League. The inaugural final was held on 20 December 2014 with Atlético de Kolkata becoming champions after defeating Kerala Blasters 1-0 at the DY Patil Stadium with the winning goal by Mohammed Rafique. Since the league's inaugural season, two teams have been crowned champions. Atlético de Kolkata won the title in the inauguration season and second time in the 2016 season. Two titles in three years meant that they have the most championships in ISL history. Chennaiyin were the only other club to be crowned champions after they won in 2015.

Team ownerships have seen some change in the subsequent two editions of the Indian Super League as Kerala Blasters now see Sachin Tendulkar teaming up with Hyderabad businessman N Prasad and film stars Chiranjeevi, Nagarjuna and Allu Arvind. Atletico de Madrid have exited the franchise having their shares bought by Sanjiv Goenka. Pune City FC has seen film star Hrithik Roshan and Serie A side Fiorentina rethink their commitment to the franchise over a long period of time. Shillong Lajong exited the Guwahati franchise after the first year of the Indian Super League. FC Goa owners Dattaraj Salgaocar and Srinivas Dempo also offloaded their stake in the club to the Deltin Group.

FOURTH HIGHEST LEAGUE AVERAGE ATTENDANCE IN THE WORLD AND IMPRESSIVE PRIZE MONEY

The number one goal for organisers of the Indian Super League was to bring football fans back to the stadium. The organisation of matches and the actual conducting of the games at the stadium have been high points of the Indian Super League with their organisation presenting fans with a great experience on the day of the match.

With a fixed time-slot of 7 pm (which in India is almost a prime time slot), the ISL registered with the audiences not only in the games but on television too. The average attendance for the Indian Super League in 2014 was 24,357 which went up to 27,111 in the 2015 season.[1]

Kerala Blasters (52,008) and Atletico de Kolkata (50,707) led the way as crowds began thronging the football stadiums to catch their favourite footballers in action. The timing and organisation made it possible for families and fans to get to the grounds, having previously skipped football games which were played at erratic times.

While in 2016 the average attendance fell partly because ATK had to move from an under-construction Salt Lake Stadium to a smaller Ravindra Sarovar Stadium, and Mumbai City moved into the heart of the city making Andheri Sports Complex their home ground—numbers have been impressive and rank amongst the best in the world in terms of the games attended.

The fact is that ISL attendance was lower only to the German Bundesliga, English Premier League and Spanish La Liga. By virtue of average attendance, the league currently stands as one of the biggest in the world. Backed by a huge marketing effort through mass media pushed by the Star Group's massive reach, the Indian Super League has created resonance with the sports loving audience

---

[1] https://en.wikipedia.org/wiki/Indian_Super_League_attendance

in the country. A league attendance bigger than France, Italy, Brazil, Argentina and China—countries that have an established football tradition is a testimony to that.

ISL's prize money is by far the best compared to any other domestic tournament in India. Only IPL, the cricket extravaganza boasts of better prize money than ISL. The Indian Super League winner gets a whooping INR 8 crores whereas the Runners-up bags 4 crores. ISL outplays the other domestic football tournament I-League where the winner bags INR 1 crore.

THE SEASONS

2014: The 2014 Indian Super League season was the first season of the ISL. The season featured eight teams, each playing fourteen matches during the regular season. The regular season started on 12 October when Atlético de Kolkata defeated Mumbai City 3-0 at the Salt Lake Stadium. The season ended on 20 December when Atlético de Kolkata defeated the Kerala Blasters in the Final 1-0.

Mohammed Rafique was the lone goalscorer when the Kolkata club became the inaugural champions. Chennaiyins Brazilian marquee player finished the season as the top goalscorer, as Kerala's Iain Hume won the 'Most Valuable Player Award'. The current Indian International, Sandesh Jhingan, was the 'Young Player of the Tournament'.

2015: The 2015 Indian Super League Season was the second season of the ISL. The season featured eight teams. The regular season kicked-off on 3 October and ended on 6 December, while the final phase began on 11 December, which concluded with the final match on 20 December. Defending champions Atlético de Kolkata were eliminated in the Semi-finals by Chennaiyin. The Final was played between Goa and Chennaiyin on 20 December 2015 at the Fatorda Stadium in Goa.

Chennaiyin were crowned as champions defeating Goa 3-2 in the Final with John Stiven Mendoza, Chennaiyin's mercurial Columbian striker rallying the team in a historic comeback.

2016: The third season of the Indian Super League began on 1 October and ended on 4 December. The final phase began on 10 December and concluded with the final on 18 December. The defending champions coming into the season were Chennaiyin.

At the end of the season, Atlético de Kolkata came out as champions after defeating the Kerala Blasters in a penalty shootout, 4-3, during the Final. The match had ended 1-1 after ninety minutes and extra time. Former Chelsea player Florent Malouda stood out for his performance for the Delhi Dynamos and he was later awarded the 'Hero of the League' award.

2017: Season four saw ten teams with new entrants Bengaluru and Jamshedpur coming in. Bengaluru was the brightest through the league phase even as FC Goa kept its attacking philosophy intact. Chennaiyin and Pune City made up the final found with North-East United and ATK finishing at the bottom of the table.

Bengaluru met FC Pune City's challenge and Chennaiyin's strong defence ensured they got the better of FC Goa's attack. Bengaluru, who were expected to win the championship, met a resolute Chennaiyin whose super set-piece routine saw them take the championship from the former's home ground.

WAY FORWARD FOR THE INDIAN LEAGUES

India Super League exceeded the television ratings, social media interactions and overall expectations of pundits and of the domestic I-League during its first three seasons. However, the league still drew criticism in other areas.

Indian players playing for both ISL teams and I-League clubs suffered from lack of visibility compared to the ones playing for ISL. In June 2017, IMG–Reliance, the AIFF, I-League representatives and the AFC met in Kuala Lumpur in order to find a new way forward for Indian football.

Although, I-League clubs East Bengal and Mohun Bagan wanted a complete merger of the ISL and I-League, the AIFF proposed that both the Indian Super League and I-League run simultaneously on a short–term basis, with the I-League winner qualifying for the AFC Champions League play-off and the AFC Cup qualification spot going to the ISL champion. The proposal from the AIFF was officially approved by the AFC on 25 July 2017, with the ISL replacing the domestic cup competition—the Federation Cup.

A month earlier, on 11 May 2017, the ISL organisers started to accept bids for two–three new franchises for the 2017–18 season. The bids were for ten cities—namely Ahmedabad, Bengaluru, Cuttack, Durgapur, Hyderabad, Jamshedpur, Kolkata, Ranchi, Siliguri and Thiruvanathapuram.

On 12 June, I-League side, Bengaluru FC and Tata Steel (for Jamshedpur) had won the bidding for new teams. Since the 2017–18 season, the Indian Super League has been running from November to March.

TEAM DETAILS

Currently, the Indian Super League consists of ten teams from nine different states in India. The league features two main derbies—the Southern Derby between Chennaiyin and the Kerala Blasters, and the Maharashtra Derby between Mumbai City and Pune City.

Club	City	Stadium	Capacity	Year of Joining	Head Coach
Atlético de Kolkata	Kolkata, West Bengal	Salt Lake Stadium	80,000	2014	Steve Coppell
Bengaluru FC	Bengaluru, Karnataka	Sree Kanteerava Stadium	24,000	2017	Carles Cuadrat
Chennaiyin	Chennai, Tamil Nadu	Jawaharlal Nehru Stadium	26,976	2014	John Gregory

Club	City	Stadium	Capacity	Year of Joining	Head Coach
Delhi Dynamos	Delhi	Jawaharlal Nehru Stadium	34,230	2014	Josep Gombau
Goa	Margao, Goa	Fatorda Stadium	19,088	2014	Sergio Lobera
Jamshedpur FC	Jamshedpur, Jharkhand	JRD Tata Sports Complex	60,000	2017	Cesar Ferrando
Kerala Blasters	Kochi, Kerala	Jawaharlal Nehru Stadium	61,148	2014	David James
Mumbai City	Mumbai, Maharashtra	Mumbai Football Arena	7,690	2014	Jose Costa
North-east United	Guwahati, Assam	Indira Gandhi Athletic Stadium	25,549	2014	Eelco Schattorie
Pune City	Pune, Maharashtra	Balewadi Stadium	9,110	2014	Miguel Angel Portugal

MOST APPEARANCES (AS OF END OF SEASON 2017-18)

1. Iain Hume (Kerala Blasters and ATK) 59
2. Sandesh Jhingan (Kerala Blasters) 58
3. Mandar Rao Desai (FC Goa) 57
4. Subrata Paul (Mumbai City FC, North-East United and Jamshedpur FC) 55
5. Narayan Das 55

TOP GOALSCORERS

1. Iain Hume (Kerala Blasters, ATK and Pune City) 28 goals
2. Jeje Lalpekhlua (Chennaiyin) 23 goals
3. Sunil Chhetri (Mumbai City FC and Bengaluru FC) 21 goals
4. Coro (FC Goa) 18 goals
5. Marcelinho (Delhi Dynamos and FC Pune City) 18 goals

THE BIGGEST STARS OF THE INDIAN SUPER LEAGUE

The Indian Super League has seen its fair share of top football players plying their trade in the country. Some exceptional footballers, though fairly late on in their careers, have come down to play for teams in the Indian Super League. The jury could be out on what their contribution is or was to Indian football, but there is no denying that they have attracted great eyeballs for the sport.

Alessandro Del Piero

The maestro made his presence felt in the very first season of ISL when he donned Delhi Dynamos' jersey. The former Juventus star was not only the marquee player for Delhi Dynamos in the first season, the Italian player was Indian Super League's premier attraction. His signing grabbed eyeballs and brought ISL to the attention of the world. Del Piero was reportedly paid a staggering salary of 10.8 crores in 2014—making him the highest paid player in the history of Indian football. The star dazzled at times and caught the eye and imagination of the football-loving audience wherever he went to play for the team.

Nicolas Anelka

The star journeyman arrived in India for the inaugural season of the Indian Super League in 2014. He was Mumbai City's marquee signing for the first season. He became the club's player-cum-manager in the following season. While he showed glimpses of his supreme self in the first season of the ISL, it would be fair to say Anelka could not really bring his A-game to the country and largely underperformed both as a player as well as a manager.

Diego Forlan

Mumbai City reportedly vied for Diego Forlan's signature for two years before finally landing their man in 2016. The 2010 World Cup's Golden Boot winner arrived last season and instantly became a huge hit as his goals and leadership took Mumbai City FC to their first ever Semi-finals appearance on the back of two very disappointing seasons.

Dimitar Berbatov

The most exciting signing for the 2017–18 of the ISL, the Bulgarian had penned a one season deal with Kerala Blasters. Things didn't shape up the way they were supposed to and Manchester United's star man spent sometime playing in the middle of the ground rather than up top. One of the most anticipated moves in the history of Indian Super League didn't quite work out the way it was planned.

Robbie Keane

The Northern Irish Forward is one of the most eye-catching acquisitions for the 2018–19. The former Liverpool, Tottenham and LA Galaxy striker was expected to lead the line and while injuries kept him out for sometime he scored eight goals in the ISL and Super Cup.

CHAPTER 7
INDIAN NATIONAL TEAM

India went on to achieve a twenty-one-year high FIFA ranking of ninety-seven, but still did not touch the all-time high of ninety-three. Englishman Stephen Constantine was appointed as the Head Coach of Indian Men's National Football Team in January of 2015 after Dutch Coach Wim Koeverman's contract ran out. This was Constantine's second stint with the Indian National Team. By the time Stephen led India to their first encounter in March 2015, its FIFA ranking had slipped to an all-time low of 173. While FIFA ranking was not an accurate representation of a nation's success at the sport, it was not something that was way off in projecting what the country was doing in the sport.

NATIONAL TEAM: THE MIRROR FOR FOOTBALL IN INDIA

A country's national team is by far the most important tool to promote the sport in the country. India's success in cricket to a huge extent is a testimony to the popularity the sport enjoyed in the aftermath of Kapil Dev's boys winning the 1983 ICC Cricket World Cup.

A nation's football team serves two important purposes—one it measures the country's football might, and two, it serves as a shining star at the top of the pyramid for millions of young footballers to be attracted towards taking up the sport in a serious manner. India has been lucky to have some very good national teams through the history of football in India. These national teams have featured some of the best football talents that the country has produced. As of 7 September 2017, Indian Men's National Football Team was ranked 97 in FIFA rankings—the best ranking for the country in twenty-one years.

The U-17 FIFA World Cup that took place in India for the first time in October 2017 saw India participate in the tournament as the host. It was for the first time ever that India played in a FIFA World Cup of any sort.

The All India Football Federation is the guardian of the Indian National Football Teams—men, women and age-group teams. Under the global jurisdiction of FIFA and governed in Asia by the AFC, it is also part of the South Asian Football Federation. The Indian team, which was once considered one of the best teams in Asia, had its golden era during the 1950s and early 1960s. During this period, under the coaching of Syed Abdul Rahim, India won gold during the 1951 and 1962 Asian Games, while finishing fourth during the 1956 Summer Olympics.

INDIA NATIONAL FOOTBALL TEAM: PRE-INDEPENDENCE ERA

To understand football in India and the significance of the National Football Team, we have to start from the pre-independence era. India played its first game with the national team in 1938. On 3 September 1938, India played their first ever international match against Australia in Sydney. Although India had lost the match 3-5 to the mighty Aussies, their efforts were praised by everyone. Indian teams started touring Australia, Japan, Indonesia and Thailand in the late 1930s. Soon after the success of several Indian football clubs, the All India Football Federation (AIFF) was formed in 1937.

Before 1937, many Indian football clubs were formed that brought popularity to the game in India. As mentioned earlier, the British soldiers introduced football to India in the mid-nineteenth century. It spread because of the efforts of Nagendra Prasad Sarbadhikari, and in 1888, the then India's Foreign Secretary, Mortimer Durand, started the Durand Cup.

The Durand Cup is now the third oldest football competition after the FA Cup and the Scottish Cup. It was initiated as a recreation for British troops stationed in India and Royal Scots Fusiliers won the first edition of the cup. In 1893, the IFA Shield was founded as the fourth oldest trophy in the world. Calcutta, the then capital of British India soon became the hub of Indian football.

The idea of India playing as a national team instead of a colony or regimental team seemed fairly closely related to the idea of an independent nation, which was not greatly appreciated amongst the officers of the British administration.

India had to be content with its iconic clubs taking charge of the representation the country put forth in its quest for identity and recognition.

AFTER INDEPENDENCE AND THE 1950 WORLD CUP—THE NATIONAL TEAM CAME INTO BEING: THE CASE OF MISSED JOURNEY TO THE WORLD CUP

The 1948 London Olympics marked the first Olympics where India competed as an Independent Nation. Captained by the talismanic Mohun Bagan player from Nagaland, Talimeran Ao, India faced the mighty France in Round 1 of the football event at the Olympics on 31 July 1948. It was India's first major international tournament, where a predominately barefooted Indian team lost 2-1 to France in the opening match, failing to convert two penalties. Sarangapani Raman scored the only goal for India; the team consisted a healthy mix of Bagan, East Bengal and Mysore players and thus the first Indian international goal ever in the Olympics was scored. While the French Equipe Tricolore won the game, India won the hearts of the crowd of seventeen thousand attendees who had gathered at Lynn Road Stadium, Ilford.

In the aftermath of World War II and a strange geo-political situation around the world, India qualified for the 1950 FIFA World Cup Finals to be held in Brazil. This was more a result of other teams' withdrawal than actual qualification. Even as withdrawals were coming in thick and fast, fifteen teams were divided into four groups with India making it to Group 3 with 1938 Champions—Italy, Paraguay and Sweden.

Along with France who had first confirmed their participation after being invited by FIFA, and then retracted their stance, India withdrew from the event after accepting the invitation. The then governing body AIFF decided against going to the World Cup, being unable to understand the importance of the event at that time, attaching importance and weightage instead to the football event at the Olympics.

The World Cup essentially was not really known as the epitome of football success, and in the decision-making corridors of the federation, the Olympics were a far more important event. The apparent reason stated was the cost of travel and while it is said that FIFA agreed to bear a major part of the travel expenses, lack of practice time, team selection issues and valuing Olympics over FIFA World cup ultimately took precedence. There was also a suggestion that India missed out on the World Cup spot owing to the fact that Indian players played barefoot and refused to play using shoes.

Although FIFA imposed a rule banning barefoot play following 1948 Olympics where India had played barefoot—the suggestion that the Indian team refused to play because they were not allowed to play barefoot is not entirely true. According to the then Indian Captain Sailen Manna, this might have been one of the many reasons floating around to justify the decision for the country not to participate in the event. He, in fact, is supposed to have stated, 'We had no idea about the World Cup then. Had we been better informed, we would have taken the initiative ourselves. For us, the Olympics were everything. There was nothing bigger. 'Indian football would have been on a different level had we made that journey,' Sailen Manna reportedly told people in hindsight years later.

Whatever the reason might have been, India missed out on a historic World Cup participation—one that the team then might have made great use of and one that the country still seeks—a senior World Cup appearance by an Indian team. The Indian team had not made it past the first round of the FIFA World Cup Qualifiers until 2018, when they defeated Nepal 2-0 over the course of two home-and-away games.

GOLDEN ERA OF INDIAN FOOTBALL: (1951–62)

Despite not participating in the World Cup in 1950, the following years particularly from 1951–64, are usually considered the 'golden era' of Indian football. India, coached by Hyderabad City Police Head Coach Syed Abdul Rahim, became one of the best teams in Asia. In March 1951, Rahim led India to their first ever triumph at the 1951 Asian Games.

Hosted in India, the team defeated Iran 1-0 in the gold medal match to gain their first trophy. Sahu Mewalal scored the winning goal for India in that match. The 1952 Helsinki Olympics did not go as per plan though. The 1952 Helsinki Olympics saw wrestler Khashaba Jadhav pick up India's first individual medal. The 1952 Olympics football event saw India bow out in the preliminary round, suffering a heavy defeat at the hands of the erstwhile Yugoslavia. India lost by a heavy margin of 10-1 which saw them going out of the tournament. India again preferred playing barefooted which led many to believe that that might have been the reason of such a humiliating defeat. Upon returning to India, the AIFF made it mandatory for footballers to wear boots.

Post their defeat, India participated in various minor tournaments such as the Colombo Cup, which they won three times from 1953–55. In 1954, India returned to the Asian Games as defending champions in Manila. Despite their achievement in the previous edition, India was unable to go past the group stage as the team finished second in Group C during the tournament—two points behind Indonesia.

Two years later, during the 1956 Summer Olympics, India went on to achieve what is still considered as the team's greatest result. The team finished in fourth place during the Summer Olympics football tournament, losing the bronze medal match to Bulgaria 3-0. The tournament is also known for Neville D'Souza's hat-trick against Australia in the Quarterfinals. D'Souza's hat-trick was the first hat-trick scored by an Asian in Olympic history.

After their good performance during the Summer Olympics, India participated in the 1958 Asian Games in Tokyo. The team once again finished fourth, losing the bronze medal match to Indonesia 4-1. The next year the team travelled to Malaysia where they took part in the Merdeka Cup and finished as the tournament runners-up. India began the 1960s with 1960 AFC Asian Cup qualifiers.

Despite the qualifiers for the West Zone being held in Kochi, India finished last in their qualification group and thus failed to qualify for the tournament. Despite the setback, India went on to win the gold medal during the Asian Games for the second time in 1962. The team defeated South Korea 2-1 to win their second major championship.

Two years later, following the Asian Games triumph, India participated in the 1964 AFC Asian Cup after all the other teams in their qualification group withdrew. Despite their automatic entry into the continental tournament, India managed to finish as the runners-up, losing out to the hosts, Israel, by two points. This remains India's best performance in the AFC Asian Cup.

ICONS OF THE ERA

Chuni Goswami

Chuni Goswami, the legendary Indian footballer was born in Kishoreganj District of undivided Bengal (now in Bangladesh). As a striker, he played fifty international matches representing India. He made his international debut for India in 1956 during the team's 1-0 victory over the Chinese Olympic team. He went on to play for India in fifty international matches including Olympics, Asian Games, Asia Cup and Merdeka Cup. He captained India to the Asian Games Gold Medal in 1962 and Silver in the 1964 Asia Cup in Tel Aviv, and in the Merdeka Cup.

He scored thirty-two goals in his fifty appearances for India—an incredible record for his times. Balaidas Chatterjee spotted his talent on the patchy turfs of South Kolkata's Deshapriya Park.

Chuni Goswami with Pele in Kolkata in 1978

In 1946, at only eight years of age, Chuni Goswami was absorbed into the Mohun Bagan junior team. He got his first chance in the senior team in 1954 and went on to spend the rest of his career in the green and maroon of Mohun Bagan until his retirement in 1968. It was under his captaincy that Indian Football has had its finest hour till date in the 1962 Asian Games.

His performance formed a critical part of the side's success and didn't go unnoticed as he was duly honoured by being named the best Striker in Asia in 1962. The following year led to more accolades for the mercurial talent as he was bestowed with the Arjuna Award in 1963.

PK Banerjee

PK Banerjee made eighty-four appearances for India, scoring sixty-five goals during the course of his career. He was one of the first recipients of Arjuna Award, when the awards were instituted in 1961 and was awarded the prestigious Padma Shri in 1990 while being named 'Indian Footballer of the twentieth century' by FIFA. His debut for the national team happened in the 1955 Quadrangular tournament in Dacca (presently Dhaka), East Pakistan (now capital of Bangladesh), at the age of nineteen.

Recurring injuries forced him to drop out of the national team and subsequently led to his retirement in 1967.

A few other notable players were the great Sailen Manna, Jarnail Singh, Peter Thangaraj etc.

POST THE GOLDEN ERA (1970–2000)

India returned to the Asian Games in 1966 but could not go beyond the group stage as the team finished third, behind Japan and Iran. Four years later, during the 1970 Asian Games, India came back and took the third place during the tournament by defeating Japan 1-0.

In 1974, India's performance in the Asian Games once again declined sharply as they finished the edition in last place in their group, losing all three matches, scoring two, and conceding fourteen goals in the first round. However, later showing steady improvement during the 1978 tournament, India finished second in their group of three.

India managed to win the football competition of the South Asian Games in 1985 and then again won the gold medal in 1987. The team then began the 1990s by winning the inaugural SAFF Championship in 1993. It ended the twenty-first century by winning the SAFF Championship again in 1997 and 1999.

ICONS OF THE ERA

Inder Singh

Arjuna awardee Inder Singh, also regarded as the finest Striker of the late 60s and 70s, started the Leaders Club in Punjab. He made his debut for the National Team in 1963 as the first player from

Punjab and was selected to play for the national team in the 1964 Asian Cup in Tel Aviv. He finished as joint top scorer in the tournament with two goals as India finished second.

His major success came at the Malaysian tournament, Merdeka Cup, where his performances won him a spot in the Asian All Stars XI team that played Arsenal in Kuala Lumpur. His performances also won him attention from the then Malaysian Prime Minister Tunku Abdul Rahman who asked him to play for the Malaysian national team.

Mohammed Habib

The son of legendary coach Syed Abdul Rahim from Andhra Pradesh is another name which had entertained Indian fans from the late 60s to early 80s. Habib played a very important role in East Bengal's young team as they embarked on a memorable season.

He made his way into Kolkata football along with Shyam Thapa, Sayeed Nayeemuddin and Afzal when East Bengal were looking for fresh blood. East Bengal won the league title that very season clinching it on the very last day, preventing Mohun Bagan from touching a unique record. Habib impressed Kolkata football by scoring for his team in the very first Kolkata Derby of his career.

Krishanu Dey

Krishanu Dey has been one of the best Midfielders India has ever had. He had a unique playing style with excellent technique and sudden burst of acceleration—a combination which enabled him to beat the opposition defender.

He represented India in ten 'A' list matches and scored seven goals—five including a hat-trick in Merdeka Tournament in Malaysia, 1986. He took part in Asian Games, Merdeka Cup, Pre-Olympics, SAFF Games and Asian Cup as a member of the Indian team. He was the captain of the Indian team in 1992 Asian Cup.

Bhaichung Bhutia

Possibly the most recognised name in the Indian football circles in the past thirty years, Bhaichung Bhutia has been considered as the torchbearer of Indian football in the international arena and nicknamed the 'Sikkimese Sniper' because of his goal scoring.

Three-time Indian Player of the Year IM Vijayan described him as 'god's gift to Indian football'. He made his senior international debut in the Nehru Cup against Thailand at the age of 19 on 10 March 1995. He scored for India against Uzbekistan in the 1995 Nehru Cup becoming India's youngest ever goalscorer, at nineteen.

India successfully defended their SAFF Championship title in 1999 by beating Bangladesh 2-0 in the Final in Goa with Bhaichung grabbing a goal as the tournament's most valuable player.

He also netted two goals in the Final of the 2002 LG Cup held in Vietnam in which India beat the host nation 3-2. In the 2007 Nehru Cup win he played a significant part in the final as he was involved in the build-up to N P Pradeep's winning goal as India went on to become the champions. The Sikkimese Sniper scored a goal in the final against Tajikistan, which India won 4-1 thanks to a Sunil Chhetri hat-trick—the victory also allowed them to automatically qualify for the 2011 AFC Asian Cup.

Later on, after finishing with three goals, he was also selected as the most valuable player of the tournament. The 2009 Nehru Cup was significant for him as he earned his 100th cap for India in a 2-1 win over Kyrgyzstan—becoming the first Indian player to reach this milestone. It was his first goal in this match that helped the team recover from their opening day defeat to Lebanon.

In the match against Sri Lanka, he scored an opening goal which helped India to win 3-1 and solidified their chances of reaching the final. He was adjudged as the 'Man of the Match' and the 'Player of the Tournament' as India beat Syria in a penalty shootout to win the championship. Shortly after the Asian Cup in 2011, which largely saw him on the sidelines with an injury, he announced his retirement for India on 24 August 2011 with a record of 40 goals in 104 appearances.

Bhaichung has multiple titles to his name, having played for all the big clubs in India. He was one of the few Indian players to have moved abroad having played football for English side Bury. He has been undoubtedly the most recognisable face of Indian football garnering visibility for the sport in even its lowest phase.

IM Vijayan

Inivalappil Mani Vijayan was one half of a very successful partnership with Bhaichung Bhutia for the Indian National Team in the late nineties and early 2000s. He was crowned 'Indian Player of the Year' in 1993, 1997 and 1999—the first player to have won the award multiple times. He was also awarded the Arjuna Award in 2003.

He made his debut in international football in the year 1989 and played in a number of tournaments such as Nehru Cup, pre-Olympics, pre-World Cup, SAAF Cup and SAF Games. He and Bhaichung Bhutia formed one of the deadliest forward lines the Indian football team had ever seen. He was part of the victorious Indian team in the 1999 South Asian Football Federation Cup and scored one of the fastest international goals in history during the tournament, hitting the net against Bhutan after only twelve seconds. He also finished top scorer in the Afro-Asian Games event held in India in 2003 with four goals.

He formally retired from international football after the Afro-Asian Games of 2003. He had scored forty goals in seventy-nine matches for India. He was affectionately called the Black Pearl of Indian Football.

A NEW BIRTH (2000–11)

In the 2003 SAFF Championship, the Indian team fell to Bangladesh 2-1. Later in 2003, India participated in the Afro-Asian Games, which were held in Hyderabad. Under Stephen Constantine's guidance, India defeated Zimbabwe 5-3—a team ranked eighty-five places above India in the FIFA rankings at the time and made it to the finals. This achievement made Constantine 'Manager of the Month' for October 2003 by the Asian Football Confederation. As India suffered heavy defeats during the 2007 AFC Asian Cup qualifiers, Constantine was replaced by Syed Nayeemuddin in 2005.

Former Malmö and China Coach Bob Houghton joined as Head Coach in May 2006. Houghton brought massive improvement in the team's football standing. In August 2007, Houghton helped India win the re-started Nehru Cup after India defeated Syria 1-0 in the Final. Pappachen Pradeep scored the winning goal for India in that match.

The following year, Houghton led India during the 2008 AFC Challenge Cup, which took place in Hyderabad and Delhi. During the tournament, India breezed through the group stage before defeating Myanmar in the Semi-finals. In the Final against Tajikistan, India, through a Sunil Chhetri hat-trick, won the match 4-1. The victory not only earned India the championship but it also allowed India to qualify for the 2011 AFC Asian Cup—the nation's first Asian Cup appearance in twenty-seven years. In order to prepare for the Asian Cup, Houghton had the team stay together as a squad for eight months from June 2010 till the start of the tournament—meaning the players could not play for their clubs.

India was drawn into Group C for the Asian Cup with Australia, South Korea and Bahrain, but lost all three of their matches, including a 4-0 defeat to Australia. Despite the results,

Indian players were still praised by fans and pundits for their valiant effort during the tournament.

PLAYERS WHO MADE A DIFFERENCE

Sunil Chhetri

The current Indian captain made his international debut in 2004. On 30 March 2004, Chhetri played his first game for the Indian U-20 team in the 1-0 victory over the Pakistan U-23 team in the 2004 SAFF Games in Pakistan. By June 2005, Sunil had scored his first goal for the senior India National Football Team against Pakistan.

His first international tournament was the 2007 Nehru Cup. In the opening game, India defeated Cambodia 6-0 with Chhetri grabbing a brace. He also scored a goal in the 2-3 defeat to Syria and another in the 3-0 win over Kyrgyzstan taking his tally to four for the tournament. India beat Syria 1-0 in the Final to become the first champions of the tournament since 1997. 2008 AFC Challenge Cup saw him bag four goals in the lead up to the Finals and then a hat-trick against Tajikistan which saw India qualify for the 2011 Asian Cup. 2009 Nehru Cup saw him score in the penalty shootout and India went on to win against Syria.

2011 Asian Cup saw him score in a 5-2 defeat at the hands of Bahrain—a well taken goal against the mighty South Koreans. India would eventually crash out losing all three matches but manager Bob Houghton heaped praises on Sunil, 'The thing about Chhetri is that he is a boy with a lot of steel and determination in him.'

He was named the National Team Captain for the 2012 AFC Challenge Cup qualification. He has been an influential leader for the Blues and has fifty-four goals from the ninety-five odd games that he has played for the national team. This makes him one of the highest active goalscorers in world football today. His exploits on the field got him contracts with Major League

Soccer side Kansas City Wizards in the US and Sporting Lisbon B in Portugal.

Subrata Paul

One of the best goalkeepers who ever played for India, Subrata Paul, has played for India in all age groups. He rose to prominence with the Under-23 team in the Pre-Olympic qualifiers where he pulled off three saves in a crucial penalty shootout against Myanmar, enabling India to qualify for the group stage.

In the group stage his goalkeeping abilities helped India pull off an unexpected draw at home against the formidable Iraq. In 2007, he replaced Sandip Nandy as the Indian Senior Team's number one for the Nehru Cup in 2007 where he was adjudged the best Goalkeeper in the tournament. His exceptional reflexes and his 'never say die' attitude earned him a contract with Danish Superliga Club FC Vestsjaelland in 2014. He has affectionately been given the title of 'Spiderman' by football loving fans of India.

CURRENT SCENARIO (2011 TO PRESENT)

After participating in the 2011 AFC Asian Cup, India's quest to qualify for the 2015 edition of the tournament began in February 2011 with AFC Challenge Cup qualifiers. Bob Houghton decided to change the make-up of the Indian squad, replacing many of the older players from the Asian Cup with some young players from the AIFF development side in the I-League, Indian Arrows. With a young side India managed to qualify for the AFC Challenge Cup with ease. However, Bob Houghton's contract was terminated, with former Dempo Coach Armando Colaco appointed as interim coach.

Savio Medeira was appointed Head Coach in October 2011 and led India to a SAFF Championship victory. Poor results in the AFC Challenge Cup in March 2012 saw Dutchman, Wim Koevermans, replace Medeira as Head Coach after the tournament. Koevermans' first assignment as Head Coach—the 2012 Nehru

Cup—saw India win their third successive Nehru Cup, defeating Cameroon's B-side on penalties.

In March 2013, India failed to qualify for the 2014 AFC Challenge Cup and also failed to qualify for the 2015 AFC Asian Cup. The team also failed to retain the SAFF Championship, losing 2-0 to Afghanistan in the 2013 Final. Koevermans resigned as Head Coach in October 2014. By March 2015, after not playing any matches, India reached their lowest FIFA ranking position of 173.

A couple of months earlier, Stephen Constantine was rehired as the Head Coach after having led India for more than a decade. Constantine's first major assignment back as the Head Coach for India was the 2018 FIFA World Cup qualifiers. After making it through the first round, India crashed out during the second round—losing seven of their eight matches and thus, once again, failing to qualify for the World Cup.

The ranking has since then improved drastically with some great number crunching by the operations team at the AIFF coupled with inspired performances by Constantine's wards taking India to a top 100 FIFA ranking. The Blues are also on a ten-match unbeaten streak, having beaten Macau away from home and they are a game away from qualifying for the 2019 Asian Cup.

He has been instrumental in getting a new crop of young Indian players ready, playing his style of extreme work-rate football. Since taking over in January 2015, he has handled thirty-five debuts in the Indian National Team—players such as Jeje Lalpekhlua, Pritam Kotal, Sandesh Jhingan, Anas, Halicharan Narzary, Rowlin Borges, Eugeneson Lyngdoh amongst many others—finding themselves as an important part of the Constantine revolution.

WOMEN'S NATIONAL FOOTBALL TEAM

With minimum input and practically no international football, the eves seemed to be a better bet competing against the best in the world. The Indian Women's National Football Team is controlled by the All India Football Federation and represents India in women's international football competitions.

The women's team resumed playing on 7 September 2012 after nearly a year-long gap of playing no international football. Interestingly, the women's team ranks way higher than the men's team in their respective FIFA rankings. Women's team ranks fifty-sixth now whereas the men's team is hovering around the top 100 mark. The first manager of the women's national team was Sushil Bhattacharya in 1975. Indian women were runners-up to Chinese Taipei women's national football team in 1979 and to Thailand women's national football team in 1983 in AFC Women's Asian Cup. These two outings were India's best record at AFC Women's Championship till date.

The Indian team also participated in the qualifiers for the 2012 Olympics. In their first match, they beat rivals and group hosts Bangladesh 3-0. In the second round, India's team played Uzbekistan where they tied the first match 1-1, but lost the second leg 1-5, and were officially knocked out. Later, Indian team earned massive success in SAFF competitions. They won the SAFF Women's Championship four times in a row without losing a single game. India won four consecutive SAFF Championships—in 2010, Bangladesh, 2012, Sri Lanka, 2014, Pakistan and 2016, India. Additionally, they won two gold medals at the South Asian Games.

With a recently established league for women in India it is only a matter of time and regular international football action that the Indian women will be a force to reckon with on the world stage. With little support and even lesser international friendlies and tournaments, the Indian Women's National Team has over the years seen great growth at the competition level. One can only imagine what some more input can bring to this sphere of football in India.

THE ICONS

Oinam Bembem Devi

Bembem Devi began training as a footballer in 1988 with the United Pioneers Club in Imphal. In 1991, she was selected to represent the Manipur U-13 team in the sub-junior football tournament. Her performances in the tournament were noticed, and she was signed by Yawa Singjamei Leishangthem Lekai club, and two years later, by the Social Union Nascent (SUN) club.

She is a regular member of the Manipur State Football Team for women since the year 1993. As the captain of her state team since the 32nd National Games, she led her state Hyderabad to victory. On 9 June 2014, Maldivian football club New Radiant signed Devi and another Indian youngster Lako Phuti. She was the top scorer of the tournament with six goals in just three matches. She was awarded the 'Player of the Tournament' for her excellent performance.

Her international debut happened at the age of fifteen against Guam in the Asian Women's Championships. The 1996 Asian Games were a turning point in her career. Her team lost to Japan 1-0 but won against Nepal 1-0 to progress from the group with Japan. Although they lost all their matches but it set the stage for Oinam Bembem Devi at the national level.

She received the armband of the Indian contingent in the AFC qualifying competition held in Thailand in 2003. She remained the captain of the Indian team that won the 11th South Asian Games held in Bangladesh, in 2010, and the 2012 SAFF Women's Championship held in Sri Lanka. She played her last game for the country on 15 February 2017 against Nepal, at the 12th South Asian Games in Shillong.

Sasmita Malik

She was awarded the 'Women Player of the Year' in 2016 by AIFF. She started playing for India in 2007 and has played thirty-five games so far. She has scored thirty-two goals for India.

Born in a small village called Aul in the Kendrapara district in Orissa, it was Devendra Sharma, the present MLA of Aul who discovered and encouraged Malik to pursue football. She joined the Bhubaneswar Sports Hostel, which became the platform for her to join the national side. In 2004, glimpses of her exceptional talent impressed all when the team was touring China.

Apart from captaining Indian Women's National Football Team several times, she has been playing for the Senior National Team since 2007, was part of the 2010 South Asian Games and back-to-back SAFF Women's Championship winning squads.

OTHER NOTABLE INDIAN WOMEN FOOTBALLERS

- Ngangom Bala Devi
- Sangita Basfore
- Aditi Chauhan
- Dalima Chhibber
- Yumnam Devi
- Loitongbam Devi
- Okram Roshini Devi
- Tuli Goon
- Dangmei Grace

PERSONS OF INDIAN ORIGIN (PIO) PLAYING FOR INDIA

India has stringent laws and criteria that determine the eligibility of sportspersons representing India. The Indian National Football Team too follows those eligibility rules while choosing its squad of players.

The rules state that only a citizen of India can be selected in the national team. Therefore, for Persons of Indian Origin or Non-Resident Indians, it is almost impossible to represent the colours of India in international football.

Former Premier League striker Michael Chopra and current Wolverhampton Wanderers captain Danny Batth are the most high-profile victims of India's stringent citizenship laws. Both, as well as many others have expressed interest in playing for India, but the rulebook does not allow their participation.

The current Indian National Team Head Coach Stephen Constantine also attests to the fact that bringing in foreign-based Indian-origin players will only help accelerate the growth of the national team as well as football in India. After all, nothing is more contagious than success.

Constantine states in his recently-released autobiography, 'They [Indian-origin players] would improve the [Indian] squad and set the bar higher for domestic players.' He suggests that not everyone is opposed to the idea of roping in PIOs and NRIs for the Indian team.

CHAPTER 8
AIFF AND OTHER FEDERATIONS

The All India Football Federation (AIFF) is the governing body of football in India. Founded in 1948, the AIFF was incidentally one of the founding members of the Asian Football Confederation (AFC) and is also a member of the South Asian Football Federation (SAFF). However, it is a relatively young federation compared to the other national football associations all over the world.

Before the AIFF came into being, the precursor to the AIFF was the Indian Football Association (IFA), which wielded immense power in the late nineteenth and early twentieth centuries in the Indian football quarters. Kolkata was the capital of the British Empire then and saw the advent of football in India. The IFA operated out of Kolkata—the nerve centre of Indian football—right from the day football got kicking in India. All decisions were taken in and around the city of Kolkata, in a fairly organised manner by the IFA. While football in India was not a nationwide phenomenon, its association too, in essence, did not control football across the country, and was more focused in the region of Kolkata and around.

Established in 1893, quite a while after the British introduced the game to India, the IFA took over the reins of football in the country during the period of colonialism.

Former England international Elphinstone Jackson was one of the founding members of the IFA. The British occupied positions in the IFA and were the sole decision-makers in the early days. It was affiliated to the Football Association in England and all foreign teams looking to play in India coordinated with the IFA. It hence, while not being a pan-India association, became the de-facto association for football in India.

The first Indian member of the IFA was Kalicharan Mitra[1] from Sovabazar Club. Sovabazar Club holds the distinction of being the first native team to topple a British team when it beat East Surrey Regiment in the 1892 Trades Cup. The British

---

[1] https://www.saddahaq.com/the-birth-of-the-all-india-football-federation

influence in the IFA continued well into the twentieth century and the body became the premier football association of India.

The IFA was based in erstwhile Calcutta—the power centre of football in British India. Hence, it harboured ambitions of becoming the controlling body for the whole of India. As such, different regional bodies came together, but there was no consensus at the end of it.

THE FORMATION OF AIFF

In the early decades of the twentieth century, very few associations were present in the various regions of India. There was no effort made by anyone to form a national body that would look after the sport across the country. It is believed the IFA felt the need to have a pan India federation and therefore invited representatives of other provincial football associations to the 1935 Darbhanga conference, which was presided over by the Maharaja of Santosh, the then President of the IFA.

Representatives of IFA—Assam, Bihar, UP, Delhi, Mysore and Bombay were present. No consensus was reached, and due to differences of opinion, the IFA delegates SN Banerjee and Pankaj Gupta left in protest, along with the Maharaja of Santosh. The remaining delegates, however, formed a body calling it 'All India Football Association'. The IFA and the Army Sports Control Board did not join this body, and a deadlock came about. The IFA tried to resolve the deadlock and sent Pankaj Gupta to Delhi for a meeting with Brigadier VHB Majendine—the President of the Army Sports Control Board.

This meeting took place in early March 1937, where both drew up a formula which ultimately led to the All India Football Federation's formation.[2] It was agreed between them that a conference should be called by the Army Sports Control

---

[2] https://www.sportskeeda.com/football/a-history-of-the-all-india-football-federation-aiff

Board towards the end of March 1937 at Delhi in which three representatives of the IFA and three representatives of the All India Football Association be present with Brigadier Majendine chairing the conference.

The conference, accordingly, took place on 27 March 1937 at New Delhi. It was attended on behalf of the IFA by late SN Banerjee, Pankaj Gupta and HN Nicholls. Others who attended were the trio from AIFA—Badrul Islam (Delhi), HE Brandon (Bombay) and Rai Bahadur JP Sinha (honorary secretary). At this conference, it was agreed to liquidate the All India Football Association, and instead, to form the All India Football Federation (AIFF) with one representative from each affiliated association and two each from IFA and ASCB.

Thus came about the formation of the AIFF as we know it today. The AIFF received FIFA affiliation in 1948 which immediately allowed India to participate in the Olympics football tournament the same year. At the London Summer Olympics in 1948, India was among the eighteen participating nations in the football tournament.

On 31 July 1948, India took another giant leap into the football elite when it took to the Cricklefields Stadium in Ilford against France in the first round of London's 1948 football tournament. Led by players like Talimeran Ao, Sailen Manna and Sahu Mewalal, India put up a spirited fight before going down 1-2 to an 89th minute René Persillon goal for France.

While the 1948 London Olympics were not a FIFA event, it was India's first appearance at a global international tournament. Since then, India hasn't participated in an event of worldwide importance until FIFA U-17 World Cup came about.

The custodians of Indian football have changed over its history of more than a hundred years. The power shift from the British dominated IFA to the formation of the AIFF in 1937 and its eventual entry into FIFA in 1948 to the current day where India is all set to play at a FIFA World Cup has happened under ten different AIFF presidents and numerous other presidents of IFA.

The 'new generation' India won the SAFF Suzuki Cup. Trivandrum, 2016
(Credit: AIFF Media)

Legends of the game: Bhaichung Bhutia has been the most recognised face of Indian Football (Credit: AIFF Media)

India retained the SAFF Women's Championship in 2016 and have won the championship 4 consecutive times *(Credit: AIFF Media)*

India qualified for AFC Asia Cup 2019 held in UAE by topping their pool *(Credit: AIFF Media)*

Stephen Constantine's second stint as national team coach saw India successfully climb up the FIFA Rankings *(Credit: AIFF Media)*

National team Captain Sunil Chhetri has been India's talisman having scored over 60 goals for the country *(Credit: AIFF Media)*

Gurpreet Singh Sandhu became the first Indian to play in a Europa League game when he turned out for Norwegian side Stabaek *(Credit: AIFF Media)*

Goalkeeper Subrata Paul was given the nick-name 'Spiderman' by the media at Asia Cup 2011 *(Credit: AIFF Media)*

Indian origin footballer Danny Batth having won the English Championship with Wolverhampton Wolves hopes to don the Blue of India *(Credit: Sam Bagnall AMA Photography)*

Football has been used as a social tool for leadership and lifeskills. A still from Goals for Girls Leadership Summit *(Credit: AIFF Media)*

Logo unveiling of the FIFA U-17 World Cup India 2017 in the presence of FIFA President Gianni Infantino, AFC President Shaikh Salman Bin Ibrahim Al-Khalifa, Mr Vijay Goel and Mr Praful Patel *(Credit: AIFF Media)*

Mr Praful Patel and Mr Vijay Goel unveil the official mascot 'Kheleo' for the FIFA U-17 World Cup India 2017 *(Credit: AIFF Media)*

India U-17 Team's playing XI historically lines up before the game against USA in New Delhi *(Credit: AIFF Media)*

Prime Minister Narendra Modi at the FIFA U-17 World Cup 2017 opening game *(Credit: AIFF Media)*

Midfielder Jeakson Singh scores India's first ever goal at a World Cup, a header against Colombia in the 2nd group game *(Credit: AIFF Media)*

FIFA U-17 World Cup 2017 Champions: England *(Credit: Khel Now)*

Sahu Mewalal's strike helped India beat Iran in the finals of Asian Games 1951

The ten men[3] who have held the post of calling the shots in Indian football:

1. Brigadier VHB Majendine (ASCB)
2. Brigadier Dorman Smith (ASCB)
3. D Moir (Bombay)
4. Pankaj Gupta (IFA)
5. Moinul Huq (Bihar)
6. M Dutta Ray (IFA)
7. Nurul Amin (Assam)
8. K Ziauddin (WIFA)
9. Priyaranjan Dasmunshi (Women's Football Association and Bihar)
10. Praful Patel (WIFA)

---

[3] https://www.saddahaq.com/the-birth-of-the-all-india-football-federation

Apart from the Presidents, the AIFF has also had twelve secretaries in its sixty-nine year history, with Kushal Das the current office bearer as the AIFF general secretary and Praful Patel as the incumbent AIFF president.

The List of AIFF Secretaries

1. Major AC Wilson (ASCB)
2. Major JB Donaldson (ASCB)
3. EJ Turner (Bombay)
4. M Dutta Ray (IFA)
5. Major Lachman Singh (ASCB)
6. K Ziauddin (WIFA)
7. Vijayrangam (Mysore)
8. Ashok Ghosh (IFA)
9. PP Lakshmanan (Kerala)
10. KN Mour (Assam)
11. Alberto Colaco (Goa)
12. Kushal Das

The AIFF has set[4] itself certain statutes and provisions.

General Provisions

1. The AIFF is a National Association registered with the Registrar of Societies, Mumbai, under the Societies Registration Act 1860.
2. The Headquarters of the AIFF are in Dwarka, New Delhi.
3. AIFF is neutral in matters of politics and religion and prohibits any form of political, religious, sexual, ethnic, linguistic, regional or racial discrimination.
4. AIFF is formed for an unlimited period.

---

[4] https://www.the-aiff.com/gerneral-body.htm

5. AIFF is a member of FIFA, AFC and Indian Olympic Association and is self-obliged to respect the statues, regulations, directives and decisions of FIFA and AFC and to ensure that these are also respected by its members.

Objectives

1. To improve and popularise the game of football constantly and promote it throughout India in the light of its unifying, educational, cultural and humanitarian values, particularly through youth and development programmes in urban, rural and remote areas, including schools, colleges and universities.
2. To organise its annual domestic and international competitions.
3. To draw up regulations and provisions and ensure their enforcement.
4. To control every type of association football including friendly matches by taking appropriate steps to prevent infringements of statues, regulations or decisions of FIFA, AIFF or of the laws of the game.

Organisation

1. The General Body is the Supreme and Legislative Body.
2. The Executive Committee is the Executive Body.
3. The General Secretariat is the Administrative Body.
4. Standing and ad-hoc committees advise and assist executive committees in fulfilling its duties.
5. Disciplinary Committee, Appeals Committee, Players' Status Committee and the Arbitration Tribunal are the judicial bodies of the AIFF.

Members of the AIFF General Body

1. One football association in each state or union territory as defined by the Constitution of India.

2. Services Sports Control Board and Railways Sports Promotion Board.
3. Women's Committee.

The AIFF undertakes various initiatives ranging from player development at grassroots level to coaching and refereeing education. FIFA's development activities are also implemented in India with the help of AIFF. At a regional or state level, AIFF's goals are taken care of by the state associations.

CHAPTER 9
INITIATIVES TO BOOST THE GAME

Football has been used as a tool for leadership, life skills, literacy, women's rights and fight against poverty. It is a strong force to affect lives in many ways other than just on the field.

TATA FOOTBALL ACADEMY

A programme and project that possibly has contributed to Indian football more than any youth development programme till date is Tata Football Academy or TFA—arguably one of the best football academies in the country. It was formed with the idea of giving a huge pool of talented players for the domestic football circuit.

'Catch Them Young' is what TFA's inherent belief is. TFA spots the best talents in the country at an early age and trains them with modern techniques, tactics, physical and mental conditioning and valuable inputs. JRD Tata's thought was to have sports as an integral part of Tata Steels. This eventually sparked the formation of the Tata Football Academy, with personal interest being taken by the then chairman of the company. The academy, conceived in 1983 and eventually launched in 1987, saw its first batch pass out in 1992, and ever since has been producing Indian internationals who have made the nation proud.

Facilities at the academy include a 100 × 65 m floodlit playground, a gymnasium, a swimming pool and recreation rooms. The rooms for the cadets are fully furnished and have all modern conveniences and facilities. There are video-aided lecture rooms and physiotherapy and fitness monitoring are taken care by well-qualified medical staff.

Special attention is paid to the nutrition and psychological advancement of players so that they can cope with stress and pressures. Through the 1990s and 2000s almost half the Indian National Team had players from the Tata Football Academy as TFA continued churning out champions serving the nation and football.

Former India international Renedy Singh is extremely proud to be an alumnus of the academy. Speaking to www.goal.com in 2014, Renedy spoke highly of his alma mater. 'TFA in our time was the best. I was there for six years and trained under Ranjan Chowdhury and Habib Sir. Those days we used to beat East Bengal, Mohun Bagan and play against so many players of the Indian team. Whatever little we have achieved is all because of them and TFA.'[1]

In the absence of a recognised youth development programme in the country, TFA cadets became extremely popular for clubs as new recruits. With the advent of AFC guidelines of extreme focus on the youth development programmes associated with clubs and also setting up of National Age Group Elite academies contribution might have dwindled a bit but the contribution to football and nation by TFA will always be memorable.

With Jamshedpur FC all set to play the ISL as a professional club, TFA will serve as their youth development programme ensuring that the TFA cadets move into the club for their professional careers. TFA's list of India Internationals is extensive having given more than 130 Indian international players of various age groups across the history of the academy's being.

The list includes the likes of Carlton Chapman, Dipendu Biswas, Mahesh Gawli, Noel Wilson, Clifford Miranda, Syed Rahim Nabi, Subrata Paul, Malsawmtluanga, Gouramangi Singh, Harmanjot Khabra, Ongnam Milan Singh, Narayan Das, Robin Singh, Pronoy Halder, Rino Anto, Udanta Singh, Konsham Chinglensana Singh and many others.

SPORTS FOR BETTERMENT

Many organisations in India have taken up sports, especially football, for the betterment of the youth. These organisations use the popularity the game enjoys with young people of all age

---

[1] http://www.goal.com/en-india/news/136/india/2012/03/20/2978026/the-tata-football-academy-indias-prime-supply-line-of-future

groups to formulate programmes for the general good of the society and the youth.

SLUM SOCCER

In 2016, *Sairat* was the biggest blockbuster in Marathi cinema grossing over INR 100 crores at the Box Office, in the process becoming the first Marathi film ever to cross that landmark. National award winning director Nagraj Manjule's reported Hindi cinema debut will feature none other than Amitabh Bacchhan, essaying the role of the founder of Slum Soccer, Vijay Barse.[2]

A story so extraordinary, it took almost eighteen years to finally come on screen. In India, a story that finally makes it as a motion picture is definitely worth special notice.

Professor Vijay Barse, a former University sports superintendent, started Slum Soccer in 2001 as 'Jhopadpatti Football'. On his way home one day, he saw kids in a slum blissfully playing football with a broken bucket. It is from there that the journey of Slum Soccer began.

The first effort was of getting these kids to play football as a proper sport. Slum Soccer started as a tournament to get teams to play.

Mr Barse's son Abhijit Barse, a former Acumen Fund Fellow joined the programme post his PhD from the US and brought about more universally recognisable branding and communication changes to 'Jhopadpatti Football', which then became Slum Soccer.

Today almost six thousand players are part of the programme where football is used as an effective tool to keep children off the streets and impart life skills to them. Across many parts of the country it is creating opportunity for people either as players, or as coaches, helping them find a route to education and better living through football.

---

[2] http://timesofindia.indiatimes.com/entertainment/hindi/bollywood/news/amitabh-bachchan-to-play-slum-soccer-founder-vijay-barse-in-sairat-directors-film/articleshow/60289939.cms

MAGIC BUS

Magic Bus is a non-governmental organisation (NGO) in Mumbai that is working with street children. It was nominated 'Charity of the Year' at the first-ever charity awards in UK.

It backs over 3,60,000 children and 8,500 young people across twenty-two states in India. It has launched a pilot programme in the UK and was honoured for its innovative use of a mentoring model and sport-based curriculum to engage children at the Asian Voice Charity Awards 2016.

It also uses football to bring in the change. Through football, they are planning to inspire and empower poor and underprivileged children in India.

Magic Bus introduces sport into slums as a medium for bringing children from different backgrounds together, earning their trust and attention, and then imparting lessons on a wide array of subjects—from hand washing to gender equality, through participatory outdoor activities organised by local volunteers known as 'youth leaders'.

For instance, at the most basic level, children play dribbling games with a ball in an open space. While other children try to distract the dribbler, he needs to go through them. They also hold a review section. This actually teaches them to fight against the odds, to fight against all the obstacles which are preventing them to get the basic and equal rights, such as education.

YUWA

In 2008, a young American named Franz Gastler made his way from working as a CSR Consultant at Confederation of Indian Industry to teach English at Krishi Gram Vikas Kendra, Ranchi, Jharkhand.[3]

---

[3] https://www.bloomberg.com/news/articles/2011-03-31/franz-gastlers-passage-to-india

A young girl at the centre asked him to teach her football. Gastler, a Minnesota native, had been an Alpine Skiing instructor for almost twelve years, but had never played or coached football. In 2009, Yuwa was formed by Gastler with an aim to utilise football as a tool to prevent child-marriage and trafficking, prevalent in large parts of Jharkhand.

Today, 250 players are attached to Yuwa's programme and good training, nutrition and coaching is combined with great tribal genes and mentality. Yuwa has been producing women footballers every year. Out of the 250 footballers currently with Yuwa, 150 practise every day. More than 600 girls are members of Yuwa at the moment in their centre in Jharkhand.

'Society teaches girls to fit in, Yuwa coaches girls to stand out,' said Gastler whose single-minded determination has made Yuwa what it is today ably aided by his wife Rose Thompson.

With great attention on learning while playing, you'll see a lot of Yuwa players and coaches delivering TedX talks across the country. When a girl joins the Yuwa team, the result is that she becomes a more regular student through positive peer presence and players elect team captains who keep track of school attendance. Girls also work together on post school learning aided by Yuwa teachers many of whom are volunteers from across the world.

STAIRS (SOCIETY FOR TRANSFORMATION, INCLUSION AND RECOGNITION THROUGH SPORTS)

STAIRS is a not-for-profit organisation working towards sports, education, health and skill development of children across India. Started by a former cricket player Siddhartha Upadhyay, STAIRS aspires to provide an opportunity to underprivileged kids to be able to pursue a dream of sporting excellence.

The organisation is driven by the mission of facilitating the process of creating an environment for children to exercise their 'right to play' and create a support system to elevate them. Its vision is to guide youth for their holistic development by channelising their energy towards meaningful activities, thus bringing about positive and constructive thinking.

STAIRS programmes include training camps, tournaments and championships, providing a platform to these children to hone their skills and showcase their talent. STAIRS taps into the potential talent and provides opportunities to climb the stairs of social empowerment and shape character by inculcating a sense of belonging to the society. With focus on achieving Sustainable Development Goals (SDGs) through sports, over 3,00,000 children play—without having to spend anything—every day at 400 STAIRS Training Centres in over 4,000 villages across seven states in India.

KHEL DUAR

Khel Duar was a dream project of two football lovers, who dreamt of having a football team. It was founded in the year 2012. These two wanted to encourage locals to play football and excel in their lives through a football club.

In the last five years of its journey, they slowly transformed it into a structured grassroots development program with focus on the development of children and youth through the game of football. More than 2,000 children and youth are associated with Khel Duar. These kids are from North Bengal, Sikkim, eastern Bihar and southern Assam.

It prepares kids for a future through football and other self-learning opportunities. They also get healthcare and special training through camps and workshops.

CEQUIN

CEQUIN was established in 2009 by Sara Abdullah Pilot and Lora Prabhu. It is an NGO promoting the rights of girls and women in India. CEQUIN is actively promoting football for girls.

It believes that as a low cost sport, all football requires is a football and a playground to begin with, making it an accessible sport for all classes to learn and develop group dynamics, life skills and self-confidence.

Football among women has effectively shattered all stereotypes associated with this so called 'masculine' game. It encourages girls to claim their right to play outdoor sports along with boys. Added to that, a survey showed that women's football scenario at the national and international levels indicates high potential of growth and success.

GOALS FOR GIRLS

Goals For Girls journey dates back to 2006 when the US-based consultant Ian Oliver took a large portfolio of sports programmes to Africa. Ian who was also a coach shared his pictures with his U-16 girls' team and they all wanted to train with him the following year onwards. Thus began the Goals for Girls programme and the Indian chapter was then added to it.

Since 2014, a group of American girls have been visiting India for two weeks accompanied by former football superstars like Cindy Parlow Cone (who is also one of the directors) to run a life-skills and leadership programme called Goals for Girls Leadership Summit, using football as a tool.

Nearly 200 girls from all across India have come each year and participated in the programme run in partnership with Delhi-based Anglian Management Group. The girls, many of whom have never left the confines of their towns, experience different cultures and people through football.

PRIME MINISTER MODI 'BATTING' FOR FOOTBALL

When the Prime Minister of a country takes a special liking to a sport and ensures that it is promoted across the length and breadth of the country, the sport is bound to grow at an astounding pace.

South African legendary leader Nelson Mandela utilised the Rugby World Cup held in South Africa in 1995 to unite the country, which was severely affected by apartheid for a long duration of time. When the 'Springboks' won, it united a nation that had seen severe discrimination.

Prime Minister Modi has possibly realised that sports can be a great tool to unite the diversity of a great country like India, a country where youth is the present and future. The world's most popular sport has to be at the forefront of the development of the country. He has time and again put his own and his government's weight behind the sport and the hosting of FIFA U-17 World Cup is the best example of that. In his talk show *Mann Ki Baat* he has often mentioned football and its power to unite people. Some excerpts from what the Prime Minister has mentioned on *Mann Ki Baat*.

'Mission XI Million will take the beautiful game of football to at least eleven million boys and girls around the country. Children in every state, from Kashmir to Kanyakumari, from Kutch to Arunachal Pradesh will get a chance to learn, play and enjoy football. More than fifteen thousand schools around the country will be partners in this. We need the support not just of children but also of every parent and every teacher to encourage boys and girls to play football and develop both the skill and fitness. I am confident that these children will be able to take Indian football to its rightful place in the world.

It is time to herald a new time for sports. There is a renewed interest in sports in this country, especially in sports like hockey and football. It is important to take football to every village and FIFA U-17 is a great opportunity. There is a renewed interest in football in India. But should we be satisfied by just hosting it, or should we be doing more? We must strive to reach the game to every nook and corner of the country.

The World Cup is an opportunity to instil in our youth the passion and fervour for football. Due to hosting of this tournament, we will get an opportunity to create good sporting infrastructure too. This FIFA Under-17 is an opportunity for India. Send your suggestions on the Narendra Modi App for branding India on the global scale. I would like every boy and girl of the country to become an ambassador of 2017 FIFA Under-17.

My dear countrymen, there is a big opportunity for our younger generation between Navratra festivities and Diwali. FIFA Under-17 World Cup is being organised in our country. I am sure reverberations of the spirit of football will be heard all around. It will evince more interest in football in every generation. There should not be a single school or college ground in India where we will not see our youngsters play. Come on, the whole world is coming to play on Indian soil, let us make sports a part of our lives.

The country has also seen the appointment of a former Olympic medalist Rajyavardhan Rathore (Athens Olympic Silver Medalist) who has put forth a new *Khelo India* programme centred around "Athletes First". This augurs well for a country bracing up for football to take over!'

CHAPTER 10
FIFA UNDER-17 FOOTBALL WORLD CUP

The FIFA U-17 World Cup promised to spark the rise of India as a new football power centre. It certainly kick-started a process that was bound to have a knock-on effect on the country's footballing landscape. This could not have been better summed up by anyone else than the President of the All India Football Federation, Praful Patel.

Patel, who for a long period of time in the lead-up to the awarding of the hosting rights, worked actively with FIFA and the Government of India to stake India's claim at the FIFA U-17 World Cup said in an interview, 'For a country like India, the priority remains to make a mark on the world stage and the FIFA U-17 World Cup hosting rights could not have come at a better time. The very fact that our boys will be getting a chance to rub shoulders with the best in the world is amazing.'[1]

There has never been an event of this magnitude held in India. The U-17 World Cup is in FIFA's list of hierarchy the third most important tournament after the FIFA World Cup and the U-20 World Cup. While various efforts have been made in Indian football by various stakeholders to raise the profile of the sport in India, mainly through marquee events, nothing would eventually match the importance that this event would have on an India bracing up to the sport.

In a country where 50 per cent of the population is below the age of twenty-five and which by 2020 will be the youngest country in the world with an average age of twenty-nine[2]—the world's most popular sport has to find home.

---

[1] http://timesofindia.indiatimes.com/sports/football/under-17-world-cup/news/we-have-international-standard-infrastructure-now-praful-patel/articleshow/60530352.cms
[2] http://www.financialexpress.com/india-news/with-an-average-age-of-29-india-will-be-the-worlds-youngest-country-by-2020/603435/

In a modern India where youngsters are constantly seeking to move to digital modes of entertainment over sport, Narendra Modi in his August address of *Mann Ki Baat* mentioned, 'During this age of computers, the playing field is more important than playstations. Play FIFA video games but also go outside and play actual football on the field.'[3]

It is with strong reason that everyone, both within and outside the country, was counting on the U-17 World Cup to deliver the punch of football popularity in India.

BIDDING AND AIMING HIGH

We have already seen how football in India developed in different phases. From Mohun Bagan's epic IFA Shield triumph in 1911 that altered the course of the nation's history, to the advent of professionalism that truly set Indian football on the international pedestal, which has now reached a new tipping point in the form of India hosting the FIFA U-17 World Cup.

It all started in 2013 when India submitted its bid to FIFA to host the 2017 U-17 World Cup. FIFA on its part had always wanted India to do well in football. It had always supported programmes in India through the AIFF and the success of India (along with that of China) in football was probably the last frontier to be captured by FIFA.

For the U-17 bid, India had competition in the form of Azerbaijan, Republic of Ireland, South Africa and Uzbekistan when FIFA invited bids for hosting of the U-17 World Cup in May 2013. With the AIFF working hard and AIFF General Secretary Kushal Das using the good offices of Praful Patel to co-ordinate with the Government of India to guarantee FIFA certain rights and privileges

---

[3] http://www.goal.com/en-in/news/fifa-u-17-world-cup-prime-minister-narendra-modi-welcomes/1en1te59a4r4o1u2trzh3t77u0

related to the hosting of a FIFA World Cup, the stage was set for the World Cup to come home.

Seven months later, on 5 December 2013, India was announced at FIFA's executive committee meeting in Salvador, Brazil, to have won the hosting rights for the 2017 U-17 World Cup.[4] Thus began a dream that in October of 2017 saw India make history by playing in the World Cup for the very first time by virtue of being the hosts.

'India will mark its arrival on the global stage and it is ready for it,' said former FIFA General Secretary Jerome Valcke, who saluted India's hosting bid in 2014:[5] 'FIFA bidding process is an open system. India had won U-17 World Cup as it was the best project.'

HISTORY OF U-17 FOOTBALL WC

The FIFA U-17 World Cup, established and formerly known as the FIFA U-16 World Championship, first started in 1985 and has been held every two years since. Although a world championship, the FIFA U-17 World Cup derived its inspiration from Asia. It was Singapore's Lion City Cup, an Under-16 tournament started by the Football Association of Singapore in 1977, that provided inspiration to then FIFA General Secretary Joe Blatter to establish the FIFA U-17 World Cup in 1985, started back then as an U-16 event. Since the Lion City Cup was wildly successful given it was only an age-group tournament, it allowed FIFA to explore the potential of youth World Cups.

The Lion City Cup is popular even today, with youth teams of famous European and South American clubs participating in it.

---

[4] http://www.fifa.com/about-fifa/news/y=2013/m=5/news=fifa-executive-committee-fully-backs-resolution-the-fight-against-racism-2085775.html
[5] https://sports.ndtv.com/football/india-may-get-to-host-fifa-club-world-cup-1511205

English Premier League club Tottenham Hotspur's U-15 team is the Lion City Cup 2015 champion beating British rivals Liverpool in the Final.[6]

Therefore, given its Asian roots, it was perhaps fitting that an Asian country hosted the first FIFA U-16 World Championship. China was the first destination of the FIFA U-16 World Championship in 1985 and the tournament moved to Canada and Scotland in the next four years before it was rebranded as the FIFA U-17 World Championship in 1991.

The early pacesetters at the FIFA U-16 World Cup were Nigeria, who won it first in 1985, followed by Soviet Union and Saudi Arabia in 1987 and 1989 respectively. Italy staged the first ever FIFA U-17 World Championship in 1991 and the tournament carried on in the same manner until 2007, when it was once again retooled to the current incarnation of the FIFA U-17 World Cup. Nigeria, the first winner of the FIFA U-16 World Championship, has won the title a record five times, followed by Brazil, who has won it three times. Other notable winners of the FIFA U-17 World Cup include African giant Ghana, who is a two-time champion, Mexico, another two-time champion, Soviet Union, Saudi Arabia, France and Switzerland.

Before the 2017 edition, seventy-nine countries had participated at a FIFA U-17 World Cup; that number has now increased to eighty-two when India, New Caledonia and Niger joined the ranks of participants.

India hosting the U-17 World Cup in 2017 marked the fifth time an Asian country hosted the global tournament, more than any other confederation. Apart from China, Canada, Scotland, Italy and India, the other countries to have hosted the U-17 World Cup are Japan, Ecuador, Egypt, New Zealand, Trinidad and Tobago, Finland, Peru, South Korea, Nigeria, Mexico, UAE and Chile. It is perhaps symbolic that India, the country with a special affinity

---

[6] https://en.wikipedia.org/wiki/Lion_City_Cup

towards mathematics and numbers, hosted the seventeenth edition of the FIFA U-17 World Cup in the year 2017.

HOTBED OF TALENT OF TOMORROW: SOME OF THE WORLD'S BIGGEST FOOTBALLERS FIRST SHONE AT THE FIFA U-17 WORLD CUP

Any conversation with FIFA U-17 World Cup 2017 Tournament Director Javier Ceppi tends to veer towards two very interesting topics—one related to the infrastructure, the presence and absence of it and its impact towards the improvement of football in a country where Ceppi compares India to his home country Chile (their lack of infrastructure not deterring development of top talent) and the second related to the FIFA U-17 World Cup being the unveiling of the future stars of tomorrow.

Apart from reaching far-flung frontiers of world football, the FIFA U-17 World Cup has also helped unearth talented footballers who have gone on to achieve big things and greatness in the football world. The likes of Toni Kroos, Francesco Totti, Iker Casillas, Ronaldinho, Gianluigi Buffon started writing their glorious football chapters at the FIFA U-17 World Cup. All of the aforementioned have won the senior FIFA World Cup, a ringing endorsement of the fact that the FIFA U-17 World Cup is a launchpad to bigger things for footballers.

Ceppi, of course, in his trade-mark style, which is usually more matter-of-fact than emotive said in a press briefing, 'The FIFA U-17 World Cup has always been a tournament to watch for the future stars and Vinicius Junior (who was expected to join the Brazil contingent at that point) comes with already a fair bit of reputation around him. It will truly be a privilege for Indians to watch live players of his stature and will also serve as bragging rights to say "I saw him live play his first World Cup in India". There will be plenty of future stars coming this October to India and Vinicius Junior will be one of them. This is a once in a lifetime opportunity for football fans.'[7]

While the likes of Italy, Brazil, Germany have been regular entrants to the U-17 World Cup, it was the first ever appearance of India at the event. That shows India's standing in the global game, but it is a situation that promises to change.

There is more and more interest in India as a growing market for football, and it is only a matter of time until we see Indian kids growing up to rub shoulders with their elite counterparts from successful football nations on the pitch. The U-17 World Cup was a catalyst for a sea change in Indian football, and the day is not far when India will have its own Buffons and Ronaldinhos.

MISSION XI MILLION: THE BIGGEST FOOTBALL GRASSROOTS INITIATIVE IN THE HISTORY OF INDIA

Every FIFA event demands the host country to put together a legacy programme. A legacy programme is essentially a plan that ensures the success of the event, which in this case was the U-17 World Cup, which carries forward to have a greater spillover of the success of the sport across the country much after the event is over. India's legacy programme associated with the FIFA U-17 World Cup is the Mission XI Million or MXIM.

'Mission XI Million' is a school contact initiative, which led up to the highly anticipated tournament in October 2017, evolved into India's biggest outreach sporting activity ever, and hopefully left a lasting legacy after the first FIFA tournament in India. It aspired to take the beautiful game of football to at least 11 million boys and girls

---

[7] http://timesofindia.indiatimes.com/sports/football/under-17-world-cup/news/vinicius-set-to-be-most-expensive-footballer-to-play-in-india/articleshow/60437130.cms

around the country and involved more than 15,000 schools to be partner in this programme.

Prime Minister Narendra Modi's vision of a wider legacy of the U-17 World Cup has seen him promote the programme and have the government earmark ₹12.55 crores for this project.[8]

FIFA U-17 World Cup project director Joy Bhattacharya, a former noted journalist and director of Indian Premier League side Kolkata Knight Riders is a passionate advocate of the fact that the U-17 World Cup brought in a new thought to young India. He believes the World Cup's real success is not just in the event being hosted but how much it inspires the India of today to take up the sport and the thought forward. 'We want to reach each and every child across the length and breadth of the country.[9] Mission XI Million is not about coaching, it is about popularising football.'[10]

With Mission XI Million the government and the local organising committee hoped to grow the sport of football organically across India and not just across certain power bases prevalent in Indian football currently. It is an attempt at introducing football into every corner of the country in a bid to popularise the sport among young boys and girls. The stated aim of the programme is to make football the number one sport among 11 million kids.

The U-17 World Cup in India is not only about 2017. Millions and millions of Indian kids have to be introduced to the game, the fun associated with playing the sport and the opportunities that it brings. India aims to play at a senior World Cup Final soon, and the U-17 World Cup was rightly called the tipping point of Indian football by the Prime Minister. The Mission must not be

---

[8] http://pib.nic.in/newsite/PrintRelease.aspx?relid=169352
[9] http://xtratime.in/how-did-gurugram-respond-to-the-mission-xi-million/
[10] http://www.asianage.com/sports/football/150417/joy-bhattacharjya-building-indian-football-legacy-ahead-of-fifa-u-17-world-cup-2017.html

mistakenly associated with technical development of the sport—it is a tool in the propagation of the sport.

The Government, the LOC and the AIFF were the driving forces behind the U-17 World Cup. With all the support from them and from the country's power brokers, India in 2017 changed the face of India as well as Indian football for good.

★

The India U-17 team was the first team to qualify for the FIFA U-17 World Cup 2017. By virtue of being the host, India qualified way earlier than the other twenty-three teams. While India qualified in December 2013, it took until June 2017 to determine the final entrants.

Qualifying tournaments and their formats vary from confederation to confederation, and spots for confederations also differ. The AFC has four spots, which went up to five this time because of an Asian host, as do the CAF, CONCACAF and CONMEBOL. Only Europe has five spots reserved at the U-17 World Cup, while Oceania has the least number of spots with two. Qualification from Asia is taken care of by the AFC U-16 Championship, which Iraq won in 2016. The Africa U-17 Cup of Nations is the qualifying tournament for African teams, while the UEFA U-17 European Championship is its European counterpart. In North, Central America and Caribbean, the CONCACAF U-17 Championship is the qualifying tournament for the U-17 World Cup.

The OFC U-17 Championship and the South American U-17 Championship takes care of matters in Oceania and CONMEBOL respectively. Iraq, Spain, Brazil, New Zealand, Mexico and Mali flew down to India in October as the champion teams of the six confederations. Like India, Niger and New Caledonia made their first ever FIFA U-17 World Cup appearance in India in 2017. However, the pressure of expectation on fellow newcomers Niger and New Caledonia was much less than on host India, who had pinned their hopes on Head Coach Luis Norton de Matos to guide the India Colts to a respectable finish in what was the country's first ever global football appearance. And they did put up a great show.

★

INDIA U-17 NATIONAL TEAM: THE MILLENNIALS WHO KNOW NO FEAR

Norton de Matos, the Portuguese Head Coach of the U-17 Indian National Team, was appointed in March 2017 replacing German Nicolai Adams and immediately faced the unenviable task of getting India ready for the U-17 World Cup. Like Norton de Matos for India, twenty-three other Head Coaches also harboured dreams of leading their respective teams to satisfactory finishes at this event.

For teams like Brazil and Mexico, who have won a combined five U-17 World Cups, age group World Cups carry immense prestige. That they are two of the better football nations at senior level shows the importance of the U-17 World Cup. India has now woken up to the reality that a better football foundation will stand the country in good stead for success at the senior level. However, the road to greatness for India's U-17 team was a difficult one, with the bridge between India and the other top national teams a bit too far though not unrealistic.

While FIFA does not have a ranking system for youth national teams, going by the senior national team rankings, five of the current top ten national teams, according to FIFA rankings, had their U-17 teams playing at the FIFA U-17 World Cup in India. India, who was ranked ninety-seventh in the August 2017's FIFA rankings, came after eighteen of the twenty-four participating nations at the U-17 World Cup in the FIFA rankings—a pointer to the pool of talent that was showcased in India during the World Cup.

To close that gap, Norton de Matos, who took over midway through India's U-17 World Cup preparation, had overseen the India Colts' exposure tours to Europe and the Americas. Those tours which featured games against top club sides and national teams meant that the Indian team had got along well in preparation for the mega event in October. During Norton de Matos' time with the Colts, India has played big European clubs' U-17 teams and six national U-17 teams. The Colts had given a good account of themselves against teams like Benfica, Sporting Lisbon, Lazio, Alcorcon (a representative Italy side), Serbia, Macedonia, Mexico, Colombia, Chile among others. In the run up to the World Cup, India under Norton de Matos had scored forty-four goals and conceded thirty-one, suggesting that good organisation and defensive solidity would have been the team's main strengths at the U-17 World Cup, more than scoring goals.

It is often said that good attacks win games but good defences win championships. India did hope for an upset or two in the World Cup and that didn't seem beyond them during their second group game against Columbia. Against all rationale and with all our humility and realism every Indian fan had hoped and prayed for an upset and those in the stands at Jawaharlal Nehru Stadium on 9 October 2017 were very close to seeing it become a reality.

★

The initial shortlist of ten venues in the host cities of New Delhi, Chennai, Pune, Mumbai, Margao, Bengaluru, Kolkata, Kochi, Guwahati, and Navi Mumbai was announced in December 2013. Following the reception of FIFA's technical report, Kochi, Delhi, Navi Mumbai, Guwahati, Margao and Kolkata were provisionally selected as venues for the 2017 FIFA U-17 World Cup in May 2015.

The FIFA delegation visited India between 19 and 25 October 2016 to evaluate the progress made towards the preparation in each of the six stadiums. The thirteen-member FIFA team, along with ten members of the local organising committee, ratified Kochi, Goa, Navi Mumbai, New Delhi, Guwahati, and Kolkata as venues for the FIFA event.

The official emblem was launched on 27 September 2016 designed as a celebration of the country's richness and diversity of cultures, with the main elements of the Indian Ocean, the banyan tree, the kite and the starburst. Each of these elements was selected for its deep significance in the culture of the country.

The Indian Ocean that served as the base of the emblem is an integral part of the subcontinent. The banyan tree is the national tree of India, deeply rooted in the culture and ethos of the country. The kite is the symbol of freedom and fun and it represents the soaring aspirations of India's young and vibrant democracy. Finally, the starburst that sat on the top of the emblem evoked festivity and celebration, representing all the festivals that grace this multicultural country, making a statement that the FIFA U-17 World Cup would be a new festival added to all calendars.

Shaped like the FIFA U-17 World Cup trophy, the emblem combined the global look of the beautiful game with a quintessentially Indian feel. It represented what the tournament stands for.[11]

The emblem was launched in a ceremony in Goa by FIFA President Gianni Infantino, Praful Patel, Chairman of the LOC and of the All India Football Federation (AIFF), AFC President Shaikh Salman Bin Ebrahim Al Khalifa and Minister for Youth Affairs and Sports Vijay Goel.

The mascot, a clouded leopard named Kheleo, was unveiled on 10 February 2017 and official slogan 'Football Takes Over' was unveiled on 27 March 2017.

National supporters Bank of Baroda, Coal India, Hero MotoCorp, BYJU's, NTPC, Dalmia Cement joined FIFA global

---

[11] https://en.wikipedia.org/wiki/2017_FIFA_U-17_World_Cup

partners—adidas, Coca Cola, Wanda group, Gazprom, Hyundai, Qatar Airways and Visa as the sponsors for this celebrated event.[12]

★

THE INDIAN TEAM AT THE FIFA U-17 WORLD CUP 2017: NORTH-EAST INDIA THE BACKBONE OF THE INDIAN U-17 TEAM

Eight boys from Manipur, one each from Mizoram and Sikkim made the north-east of India the strongest provider of football players to the Indian National Team that represented the country at the World Cup. Bengali boys, Jitendra Singh, Abhijit Sarkar and Rahim Ali's inclusion took the number of boys from the East Zone of the country to thirteen, a majority; two each from Punjab, Karnataka and Maharashtra and one each from Kerala completed the numbers for the Indian squad. Canada-based Punjabi person of Indian origin, Sunny Dhaliwal, gave up his Canadian citizenship to be eligible to play for India at the World Cup. Similarly, New Jersey-based Maharashtrian boy Namit Deshpande, whose parents are settled in the US since 2006, was scouted by an effort of the AIFF, headed by World Cup team COO Abhishek Yadav.

Goalkeepers

1. Dheeraj Singh Moirangthem (Manipur)
2. Prabhsukhan Singh Gill (Punjab)
3. Sunny Dhaliwal (Canadian of Indian origin—took up Indian citizenship)

---

[12] http://www.fifa.com/u17worldcup/organisation/partners/index.html

Defenders

4. Boris Singh Thangjam (Manipur)
5. Jitendra Singh (West Bengal)
6. Anwar Ali (Punjab)
7. Sanjeev Stalin (Karnataka)
8. Hendry Antonay (Karnataka)
9. Namit Deshpande (New Jersey (USA)/Maharashtra)

Midfielders

10. Suresh Singh Wangjam (Manipur)
11. Khumanthem Ninthoinganba Meetei (Manipur)
12. Amarjit Singh Kiyam (Manipur)—**Captain**
13. Abhijit Sarkar (West Bengal)
14. Komal Thatal (Sikkim)
15. Lalengmawia (Mizoram)
16. Jeakson Singh Thaunaojam (Manipur)
17. Nongdamba Naorem (Manipur)
18. Rahul Kannoly Praveen (Kerala)
19. Md. Shahjahan (Manipur)

Forwards

20. Rahim Ali (West Bengal)
21. Aniket Jadhav (Maharashtra)

★

Launched by Spanish legend Carles Puyol on 16 May 2017, the general ticket sales for the U-17 World Cup had started on 17 May 2017 at 19:11 hours. The special time was selected by the organising committee to celebrate the 1911 victory of Bagan over East Yorkshire regiment.

On 6 October 2017, the U-17 World Cup kicked off at two venues with Colombia taking on Ghana in Group A in Delhi and New Zealand taking on Turkey at the DY Patil stadium in Mumbai. India who was placed in Group A played at 7 pm later in the day at the Jawaharlal Nehru Stadium in Delhi. FIFA had specially requested India not to organise an opening ceremony and instead invest the money in development of the sport in India.

Over the next twenty-three days till the Finals on 28 October 2017, India had broken the record for the maximum crowd attendance at an U-17 World Cup with the combined attendance standing at 1,347,133, surpassing China's 1985 edition where it was 1,230,976.

The young stars of England, many of whom were from the famed English premier league clubs, had trailblazed the world cup, winning the cup for the first time in the country's history.

Spain took home the runners-up trophy while fancied Brazil had to be content with a third place finish.

GROUP STAGES

Group A

India
Coach: Luis Norton de Matos
U-17 World Cup record, best result: First appearance this year.
Qualification for India 2017: Automatically qualified as hosts.
Last appearance at FIFA Under-17 World Cup, result: N/A
Key players: Amarjit Singh Kiyam, Dheeraj Singh Moirangthem, Jeakson Singh Thaunaojam.

USA
Coach: John Hackworth
U-17 World Cup record, best result: Debut in 1985, fourth place in 1999.
Qualification for India 2017: Finished in the top four at the CONCACAF Under-17 Championship 2017.

Last appearance at FIFA Under-17 World Cup, result: 2015, group stage exit.
Key players: Justin Garces, Josh Sargent, Timothy Weah.

Colombia
Coach: Orlando Restrepo
U-17 World Cup record, best result: Debut in 1989, fourth place in 2003 and 2009.
Qualification for India 2017: Finished in the top four at the South American Under-17 Championship 2017.
Last appearance at FIFA Under-17 World Cup, result: 2009, fourth place.
Key players: Juan Penaloza, Jaminton Campaz.

Ghana
Coach: Paa Kwesi Fabin
U-17 World Cup record, best result: Debut in 1989, champions in 1991 and 1995.
Qualification for India 2017: Finished in the top four at the Africa Under-17 Cup of Nations 2017.
Last appearance at FIFA Under-17 World Cup, result: 2007, fourth place.
Key players: Eric Ayiah, Emmanuel Toku.

India was placed in Group A along with Ghana, Columbia and the United States. The group was based primarily out of Delhi playing most of their games at the Jawaharlal Nehru Stadium. Ghana beat Columbia 1-0 in the first game of the group which also opened the tournament. The second game of the day saw India take on the United States. It was the first time that the Indian national anthem was played at a football World Cup. The occasion was momentous as Indian football team superstars of yesteryears were facilitated by the Prime Minister before the game.

46,351 fans gathered at the JLN were hoping for an upset of sorts. The US team included amongst others Paris St Germain's

Timothy Weah, son of former FIFA World Player of the Year George Weah who is now also the President of Liberia. For thirty minutes the Indian team battled hard before conceding a soft penalty just inside the box. Jitendra Singh's foul on Josh Sergeant got the US a penalty which was calmly slotted by the American captain. Goals by Durkin and Carleton handed India a defeat in their first ever game at the World Cup.

Indian Goalkeeper Dheeraj Moirangthem gathered a lot of praise for his stupendous display. US quickly grabbed their second win of the tournament when they beat Ghana 1-0 in their second game of the group. India playing next against Columbia in the 7 pm kick-off had 48,184 screaming Indian fans for support this time around. At 0-0 going into the break, India had raised the hopes of every fan watching in the stadium and of those following the game all across the country. A forty-ninth minute goal from Juan Penaloza however gave the Columbians a 1-0 lead.

India continued putting up a great effort to get the equaliser that would give them their first point in the World Cup. They were rewarded for their persistence when a Sanjeev Stalin corner found Jeakson Singh heading in India's first goal in a World Cup. However, almost a minute later Gustavo Carvajal's through ball found Penaloza in the Indian box and the striker's right footed shot found its way past Dheeraj into the right hand bottom corner dashing the Indian hopes.

Ghana beat a visibly tired looking Indian side 4-0 to end India's World Cup campaign without a point even as Columbia beat US 3-1 with each one of the sides qualifying for the Round of 16.

Indian campaign at the World Cup ended as the bottom placed side but the effort put in captured the imagination of every fan in the country. India's games enjoyed tremendous support with the three games garnering match attendance of 46,351 (US), 48,184 (Columbia) and 52,614 (Ghana).

Never before had the capital city of India seen fervour of this kind for football. This has to be one of the key indicators of the success that the FIFA U-17 World Cup has been.

Group B

Paraguay
Coach: Gustavo Morinigo
U-17 World Cup record, best result: Debut in 1999, quarter-finalists in 1999.
Qualification for India 2017: Finished in the top four at the South American Under-17 Championship 2017.
Last appearance at FIFA Under-17 World Cup, result: 2015, group stage exit.
Key players: Martin Sanchez, Antonio Galeano.

Mali
Coach: Jonas Komla
U-17 World Cup record, best result: Debut in 1997, runners-up in 2015.
Qualification for India 2017: Finished in the top four at the Africa Under-17 Cup of Nations 2017.
Last appearance at FIFA Under-17 World Cup, result: 2015, finished runners-up.
Key players: Hadji Dramé, Lassana N'Diaye.

New Zealand
Coach: Danny Hay
U-17 World Cup record, best result: Debut in 1997, reached last 16 in 2009, 2011 and 2015.
Qualification for India 2017: Won the OFC Under-17 Championship 2017.
Last appearance at FIFA Under-17 World Cup, result: 2015, reached last 16.
Key players: Charles Spragg, Max Mata.

Turkey
Coach: Mehmet Hacioglu
U-17 World Cup record, best result: Debut in 2005, fourth place in 2005.
Qualification for India 2017: Finished in the top five at the Under-17 European Championship 2017.
Last appearance at FIFA Under-17 World Cup, result: 2009, reached quarter-final.
Key players: Ozan Kabak, Malik Karaahmet.

Group B started on the same day as Group A with Mumbai being the headquarters of the group. Paraguay won all their games topping the group with nine points with Mali winning two of their three games to finish second in the group.

New Zealand and Turkey drew their game and ended up with one point each which saw both of them crash out of the World Cup. Paraguay-Mali game was the highlight of the group with Paraguay going into an early 2-0 lead through goals from Galeano and Sanchez in the twelfth and seventeenth minutes.

Mali, however, quickly pulled two goals back with Drame and Ndiaye getting goals in the twentieth and thirty-fourth minute. Ultimately it took a Rodriguez penalty in the fifty-fifth minute for Paraguay to take home all three points while the Mali side qualified for the Round of 16 as the second placed team.

Group C

Iran
Coach: Abbas Chamanyan
U-17 World Cup record, best result: Debut in 2001, reached last 16 in 2009 and 2013.
Qualification for India 2017: Finished in the top four at the AFC Under-16 Championship 2016.

Last appearance at FIFA Under-17 World Cup, result: 2013, reached last 16.
Key players: Younes Delfi, Alireza Asadabadi, Allahyar Sayyad.

Guinea
Coach: Souleymane Camara
U-17 World Cup record, best result: Debut in 1985, fourth place in 1985.
Qualification for India 2017: Finished in the top four at the Africa Under-17 Cup of Nations 2017.
Last appearance at FIFA Under-17 World Cup, result: 2015, group stage exit.
Key players: Djibril Toure, Elhadj Bah.

Germany
Coach: Christian Wuck
U-17 World Cup record, best result: Debut in 1985, runners-up in 1985.
Qualification for India 2017: Finished in the top five at the Under-17 European Championship 2017.
Last appearance at FIFA Under-17 World Cup, result: 2015, reached last 16.
Key players: Jann-Fiete Arp, Elias Abouchabaka.

Costa Rica
Coach: Breansse Camacho
U-17 World Cup record, best result: Debut in 1985, quarter-finalists in 2001, 2003, 2005 and 2015.
Qualification for India 2017: Finished in the top four at the CONCACAF Under-17 Championship 2017.
Last appearance at FIFA Under-17 World Cup, result: 2015, reached quarter-final.
Key players: Walter Cortes, Jose Alfaro.

Group C saw Asian powerhouse Iran being drawn into current Senior World Cup holders Germany along with Guinea and Costa Rica. The Asians shocked the footballing world handing Germany a 4-0 convincing defeat with Esteghlal Khuzestan forward Younes Delfi scoring a brace. Sayyed and Namdari added a goal each as one of the famous U-17 World Cup upsets was completed.

The press back home in Iran was more sedate though, wondering when the triumph at the U-17 level would be replicated at the senior level. This goes to show the expectations the highest ranked Asian country had from its set of footballers.

Seventeen-year-old Jann-Fiete Arp, who had two senior goals from three games with the Bundesliga side Hamburger before the world cup started, scored a goal each in Germany's wins over Costa Rica and Guinea to see to it that Germany did qualify for the next round. Both Guinea and Costa Rica failed to progress beyond the group stage.

Group D

Korea DPR
Coach: Yun Jong Su
U-17 World Cup record, best result: Debut in 2005, quarter-finalists in 2005.
Qualification for India 2017: Finished in the top four at the AFC Under-16 Championship 2016.
Last appearance at FIFA Under-17 World Cup, result: 2015, reached last 16.
Key players: Kye Tam, Kim Pom-hyok.

Niger
Coach: Tiemogo Soumaila
U-17 World Cup record, best result: First appearance this year.
Qualification for India 2017: Finished in the top four at the Africa Under-17 Cup of Nations 2017.

Last appearance at FIFA Under-17 World Cup, result: N/A
Key players: Habibou Sofiane, Abdoul Moussa.

Brazil
Coach: Carlos Amadeu
U-17 World Cup record, best result: Debut in 1985, champions in 1997, 1999 and 2003.
Qualification for India 2017: Finished in the top four at the South American Under-17 Championship 2017.
Last appearance at FIFA Under-17 World Cup, result: 2015, reached quarter-final.
Key players: Paulinho, Lincoln, Alan Souza.

Spain
Coach: Santi Denia
U-17 World Cup record, best result: Debut in 1991, runners-up in 1991, 2003 and 2007.
Qualification for India 2017: Finished in the top five at the Under-17 European Championship 2017.
Last appearance at FIFA Under-17 World Cup, result: 2009, finished third.
Key players: Abel Ruiz, Nacho Diaz.

Kochi possibly got the cream of the group action as Group D saw heavyweights Brazil and Spain drawn into the same group. The first game of the group saw Spain take on Brazil who were in the lead very soon when an own goal from Wesley saw Spain take the lead as early as the fifth minute.

Brazil who had come into the U-17 World Cup with the clear aim of winning it didn't give up and an exciting game that saw end to end action saw Lincoln equalise in the twenty-fifth minute. Vasco Da Game player Paulinho, who had earlier in the year become the youngest ever scorer in the Brazil top division Serie A, then finished off a fine move from the Brazilians in the injury time of the first half.

All efforts from Spain to get a goal in the second half proved futile as Brazil got the all important three points to kick-start their World Cup. Niger and North Korea offered little resistance to both the heavyweights as they qualified for the knockout rounds with ease. Niger beat North Korea in the other match of the group to take three points and a place in the Round of 16.

Group E

Honduras
Coach: Jose Valladares
U-17 World Cup record, best result: Debut in 2007, reached quarter-final in 2013.
Qualification for India 2017: Finished in the top four at the CONCACAF Under-17 Championship 2017.
Last appearance at FIFA Under-17 World Cup, result: 2015, group stage exit.
Key players: Carlos Mejia, Patrick Palacios.

Japan
Coach: Hirofumi Yoshitake
U-17 World Cup record, best result: Debut in 1993, quarter-finalists in 1993 and 2011.
Qualification for India 2017: Finished in the top four at the AFC Under-16 Championship 2016.
Last appearance at FIFA Under-17 World Cup, result: 2013, reached last 16.
Key players: Keito Nakamura, Takefusa Kubo, Hiroto Yamada.

New Caledonia
Coach: Dominique Wacalie
U-17 World Cup record, best result: First appearance this year.
Qualification for India 2017: Finished runners-up at the OFC Under-17 Championship 2017.

Last appearance at FIFA Under-17 World Cup, result: N/A
Key players: Paul Gope-Fenepej, Bernard Iwa.

France
Coach: Lionel Rouxel
U-17 World Cup record, best result: Debut in 1987, champions in 2001.
Qualification for India 2017: Finished in the top five in the Under-17 European Championship 2017.
Last appearance at FIFA Under-17 World Cup, result: 2015, reached last 16.
Key players: Amine Gouiri, Maxence Caqueret.

Olymipique Lyon forward Amine Gouiri's five goals saw France power their way to the top of Group E. France started the campaign with a 7-1 victory over newcomers New Caledonia in Guwahati. Japan offered some resistance to the French which was overcome with some difficulty as Gouiri got a brace for the French to triumph 2-1.

An easy 5-1 victory of Honduras closed the group engagements for France with Japan picking up the runners-up slot. Keito Nakamura emulated his famous senior namesake Shunsuke with four goals in the group stages including a hat-trick against Honduras. Honduras' 5-0 win against New Caledonia was good enough for them to seal a spot in the Round of 16.

Group F

Iraq
Coach: Qahtan Jathir
U-17 World Cup record, best result: Debut in 2013, first round in 2013.
Qualification for India 2017: Finished in the top four at the AFC Under-16 Championship 2016.

Last appearance at FIFA Under-17 World Cup, result: 2013, group stage exit.
Key players: Mohammed Dawood, Muntadher Mohammed.

Mexico
Coach: Mario Arteaga
U-17 World Cup record, best result: Debut in 1985, champions in 2005 and 2011.
Qualification for India 2017: Finished in the top four at the CONCACAF Under-17 Championship 2017.
Last appearance at FIFA Under-17 World Cup, result: 2015, fourth place.
Key players: Jairo Torres, Daniel Lopez.

Chile
Coach: Hernan Caputo
U-17 World Cup record, best result: Debut in 1993, third place in 1993.
Qualification for India 2017: Finished in the top four at the South American Under-17 Championship 2017.
Last appearance at FIFA Under-17 World Cup, result: 2015, reached last 16.
Key players: Gaston Zuniga, Alexis Castro.

England
Coach: Steve Cooper
U-17 World Cup record, best result: Debut in 2007, quarter-finalists in 2007 and 2011.
Qualification for India 2017: Finished in the top five at the Under-17 European Championship 2017.
Last appearance at FIFA Under-17 World Cup, result: 2015, group stage exit.
Key players: Phil Foden, Rhian Brewster, Jadon Sancho.

Group F saw former champions Mexico drawn up in the same group as crowd favourites England, along with Chile and Iraq. Kolkata played host to the group as England gave early indicators of their prowess as they beat Chile 4-0 in the opening game of the group.

The English youngsters played like seasoned pros with their expansive style of play, passing the ball through tight spaces and moving the ball with pace and precision. Jordan Sancho and Angel Gomes who had had senior appearances for Borussia Dortmund and Manchester United respectively took centre-stage in the group stages with Sancho getting three goals and Gomes two.

Former champions Mexico barely scraped into the next round finishing bottom of the sixteen qualifiers with two points. Iraq though were a revelation as Iraqi Premier League side Al-Naft's Mohhamed Dawood Yaseen scored first against Mexico in the first game and then followed it up with a brace against Chile sending the South Americans home.

The young prodigy has been listed in Guardians List of Top 60 young talents in world football in 2017.

ROUND OF 16

Columbia 0-4 Germany

Germany made short work of Columbia as Arp again was in fine form grabbing a brace with Bisseck and Yeboah getting one goal each. Columbian side had qualified as second placed team from India's group A and while the game was held in Jawaharlal Nehru Stadium, which they were familiar with, the German team stung by a 4-0 loss to Iran in the group stages was in an unrelenting mood and allowed no time to the Columbians to get into the game.

Paraguay 0-5 United States of America

Another one-sided affair was Timothy Weah picking up a hat-trick to hand group B winners Paraguay a tough loss which saw them crashing out of the U-17 World Cup despite showing huge promise in the Group stages. New MLS franchise team Atlanta United's Andrew Carleton and Captain Josh Sergeant were the other goal getters.

Sergeant headed to Werder Bremen after the World Cup. He received a call up from the Senior National US Men's team camp becoming the only US player ever to have participated in the U-17, U-20 and Senior Team camps in one calendar year. Such is the impact U-17 World Cup had across the world.

Iran 2-1 Mexico

Iran beat Mexico to end what could be termed an unsuccessful outing for the Central American nation at the World Cup having previously won it. Iran took an early 2-0 lead and it was always a tough task from there on for the Mexicans who did get one goal back in the first half but it was a mountain too hard to climb.

France 1-2 Spain

Two European powerhouses met possibly too early in the World Cup and the game didn't disappoint. France took the lead in a tense contest in the thirty-fourth minute through Lenny Pintor after some fine display and pass by Amine Gouiri.

Barcelona B left back Juan Miranda got the equaliser in the forty-fourth minute finishing off a great Ferran Torres cross. The game seemed to be heading into a penalty shootout when in the ninetieth minute Jose Lara was brought down by Oumar Solet in the French box which saw Spanish Captain Abel Ruiz converting to send the Spanish into the quarters.

England 0 (5)-(3) 0 Japan

Japan became the only team in the World Cup not to be beaten by England in regular time at the U-17 World Cup as 'The Nippon' produced a disciplined performance to stop a strong English side from scoring. Japan had chances by the end of the game. However, the game went into penalty shootout post ninety minutes of regulation time (U-17 World Cups don't have extra time). Cerezo Osaka midfielder Hinata Kida missed Japan's third kick as England scored all their five to advance into the quarters.

Mali 5-1 Iraq

Lassana N'diaye scored a brace as impressive Iraq couldn't replicate their group form against a strong Mali. Eventually, the Africans proved too strong and took home a five goal win.

Ghana 2-0 Niger

Goals from Eric Ayiah and Richard Danso, end of the first and second half respectively, took Ghana through to the quarters at the expense of Niger.

Brazil 3-0 Honduras

Sau Paolo Forward Brenner Souza's brace was enough to seal a 3-0 win for the mighty Brazil in the last Round 16 game against Honduras.

QUARTER-FINALS

Mali 2-1 Ghana

Heavy rains in Guwahati saw the lowest turnout for a game as Mali outclassed Ghana on a rain soaked pitch. Hadji Drame and Djemoussa Traore's goals were enough to take Mali to the Semi-finals.

Unites States 1-4 England

An injury time penalty saw Liverpool striker Rhian Brewster complete his hat-trick, and even though US got a consolation strike to a very impressive Josh Sergeant, England coasted through to the Semi-finals of the World Cup. Wolverhampton Wolves' Morgan Gibbs-White got the other goal for the three lions.

Spain 3-1 Iran

Iran were unlucky to catch Spain on one of their finest days as the Spanish passed and moved with pace and guile and outclassed a very strong Iran side 3-1 in an exciting clash in Kochi. Abel Ruiz opened the scoring in the thirteenth minute. Sergio Gomez and Ferran Torres got two quick goals in the sixtieth and sixty-seventh minute. Iran could only manage a consolation goal through Arp.

Germany 1-2 Brazil

The match of the Quarter-finals saw two of the top teams in world football play each other. Germany started on the front foot as Jann-Fiete Arp got a quick goal for 'Die Mannschaft' as the first half ended 1-0 in favour of the Germans. Weverson and Paulinho, however, got goals in the seventy-first and seventy-seventh minute for Brazil, and Germany couldn't quite recover from the quick setback which sent Brazil through to the Semis.

SEMI-FINALS

Brazil 1-3 England

Rhian Brewster show continued as the game which was originally to be played at the Indira Gandhi Stadium in Guwahati was shifted to Yuwa Bharti Kridangan in Kolkata much to the delight of the 'Mad for Brazil' Kolkata crowd. The Liverpool hitman struck thrice in the tenth, thirty-ninth and seventy-seventh minute to regale the English supporters and end Brazil's road to the Finals. Wesley's strike in the twenty-first minute had drawn parity but it was all England on the road to the Finals.

Mali 1-3 Spain

Abel Ruiz was turning out to be Spain's star man as the Barcelona B striker again turned in an impressive performance capped with a brilliant brace which took Spain to the Final to face England. Valencia B's talented winger Ferran Torres who had a fantastic World Cup till those stages capped another brilliant display with a goal to his name. Ndiaye got Mali a consolation goal but the African nation were relegated to playing the third place play-off with Brazil.

THIRD PLACE

Brazil 2-0 Mali

Brazil coasted to an easy 2-0 win over Mali with Alan Souza and Yuri Alberto getting the goals. While third place might not have been what Brazil came to India aiming for, it was in the end a decent consolation for enthralling fans with some great football.

FINALS

England 5-2 Spain

England's big day turned into a nightmare early on in the game as Spain took a two-goal lead. Sergio Gomez Martin, who still plays for Barcelona's age group teams and hasn't been promoted to the B side of the Catalan Giants, got a quick brace as the English seemed shell shocked. Rhian Brewster, however, got a goal just before halftime that gave England some hope going into halftime with a one-goal deficit.

The floodgates opened however after Gibbs White's equaliser in the fifty-eighth minute. Player of the tournament, Manchester City's Phil Foden, scored a brace quickly and Marc Guehl another as England completed a historic turnaround to capture the U-17 World Cup 2017 in India.

Rhian Brewster ended up being the top scorer with 8 goals while Brazil's Gabriel Brazao was awarded the best goalkeeper award. Phil Foden was named the Player of the World Cup and soon enough was playing games for Manchester City in the Premier League. He capped his time at City with a Premier League winners medal in 2017–18.

England went on to win the U-20 World Cup title as well and for the moment holds both the U-17 and the U-20 World Cup titles.

FIFA U-17 WORLD CUP 2017: INDIA'S FOOTBALL INFLECTION POINT

The U-17 World Cup was stated to be the most important event in the history of Indian football, as India looked forward to becoming a world power in the sport of football. The world cup has in fact brought a lot of positives to the country and it would be a good ending to this book to have a look at how the event fared.

The world cup has brought the sport to the fore as one of the most loved sports in India. A lot of media attention has also managed to attract fans whose first choice of sport was not football. For the sport to grow, it is important that it transcends the borders of limited followers of non-cricket sports.

The World Cup managed to secure one of the best fan attendances in the world as far as an U-17 World Cup is concerned.

Also *Sony's* coverage of the FIFA U-17 World Cup garnered one of the highest ratings for sport in India, much higher than an extremely popular Premier League.

India has had very little exposure to what it requires to be a top team in the world in football. The World Cup has brought Indians closer to a level where people know what it takes for India to compete at the world stage.

The senior world cup is still a distant dream for India. However, what seems to have happened post the U-17 World Cup is for young Indian players to identify themselves with Indian U-17 players such as Sanjeev Stalin, Dheeraj Moirangthem, Jeakson Singh and Amarjit Singh. The extremely important aspect for the sport in India to pick up the pace to compete with the world is identification of heroes for the younger generation. The Indian U-17 team seems to have found the answer.

Many more organisations, both in the sponsorship and development sector, are now open to including football in their list of sports that are being supported. Six Indian companies were on the list of the sponsors of the FIFA U-17 World Cup.

Probably one of the biggest positives for football now is the support that the Government provided to the World Cup. Right from support campaigns to the financial support at various levels, the Government has pushed the world cups and football's cause in India.

Mission XI Million has initiated a huge number of children into football. The goal is not excellence but interest and that is very important to build a base of the pyramid for Indian football.

With the world cup played at each one of the six venues, we now have one main stadium along with four training pitches. This pool of thirty pitches is a great resource for any further events taking place in India and has to be carefully managed and looked after while adding a lot more pitches and grounds for children to pick the game up.

ABOUT THE AUTHORS

Shantanu Gupta is an Indian author, TEDx speaker and political analyst. His latest book *The Monk Who Became Chief Minister*—biography of Yogi Adityanath, is listed as the 'Most memorable Non-Fiction Book of 2017' by Amazon. Shantanu has an engineering degree from GB Pant University, Management education from XLRI, Jamshedpur, and did his masters in policy and politics from Institute of Development Studies (IDS), University of Sussex (United Kingdom). He has worked for a decade as a process and management consultant in many cities in India, Switzerland, Cyprus, Hungry and Israel. He has represented India at many international conferences on economy and policy, in Germany, Malaysia and Sri Lanka.

Shantanu has authored three more books—*Uttar Pradesh, Vikas Ki Pratiksha Mein* (Bloomsbury), *Compilation of Prime Minister's Mann Ki Baat* (Kapot Books) and *Education Policy in India—Voice, Choice and Incentives* (CCS).

Nikhil Paramjit Sharma is the founder-CEO of zlait Sports Management and works actively in the sports consultancy, infrastructure and athlete management domain. He has also until recently served as Director on the board of Shillong Lajong Football Club—an I-League club from the North-East of India. He was part of the founding team that incepted the Guwahati franchise in the Indian Super League in 2014 which he led as Head of Football in the 2014 ISL season. A certified Football Coach with AIFF, AFC and FIFA courses attended, Nikhil is passionate about technical advancement, commercialisation and branding of the sport of football, particularly in India. He has authored numerous articles and essays relating to football in India focussing on sustainability and sports marketing.

Nikhil has been instrumental in bringing world famous sports clubs and brands to India through his entire career in sports management. He has previously worked in various FMCG, Retail and Media organisations across the length and breadth of the country. He has an engineering degree from Bharti Vidyapeeth in Pune and Management education from MICA, Ahmedabad.

Behind the seemingly ordinary life of a practising architect lies a whole host of non-professional impulses that give shape to buildings. *Stories of Storeys: Art, Architecture and the City* is about these impulses and conditions—social, literate, personal and political—which are expressed, but often ignored in architecture. Bhatia looks at the ordinary, physical, visible and tactile involvement of our urban environment and the way it affects, communicates with, or influences us.

An all-inclusive sociology of architecture through the eyes of a renowned architect

For special offers on this and other books from SAGE, write to marketing@sagepub.in

Explore our range at
www.sagepub.in

Paperback
978-93-532-8080-2

Extolled for his extraordinary courage, Bhagat Singh is one of our most venerated freedom fighters. He is valourised for his martyrdom, and rightly so, but in the ensuing enthusiasm, most of us forget his contributions as an intellectual and a thinker. In the current political climate, when it has become routine to appropriate Bhagat Singh as a nationalist icon, not much is known about his nationalist vision. This book provides a corrective to this by bringing together a majority of Bhagat Singh's writings, some of which were hitherto unavailable in English.

A collection that brings together Bhagat Singh's seminal writings

For special offers on this and other books from SAGE, write to marketing@sagepub.in

Explore our range at
www.sagepub.in

Paperback
978-93-528-0837-3

Ilaiah Shepherd's evocative memoirs reveal the struggle for education and dignity that a great majority of Indians undergo. As a little boy herding sheep and goats, he and his brother were the first in their family to go to school. The author writes of his long and often interrupted journey to becoming a writer and an intellectual, without support and having to overcome adversities. In English, this is the first written account of growing up in an OBC family and covers social issues that affect those regarded as the lower castes.

A chronicle of the author's childhood and his eventual rise as public intellectual

For special offers on this and other books from SAGE, write to marketing@sagepub.in

Explore our range at
www.sagepub.in

Paperback
978-93-81345-41-2

> This is a book written in anger—anger over the long history of oppression and ruthless exploitation under British rule. It is a scholarly work and is also a powerful political text.
>
> **Amar Farooqui**
> *Professor, Department of History, University of Delhi*

A freedom fighter's telling account of the exploitation of India by the East India Company

For special offers on this and other books from SAGE, write to marketing@sagepub.in

Explore our range at
www.sagepub.in

Paperback
978-93-528-0802-1